LIES, BRIBES & PERIL

LIES, BRIBES & PERIL

✦

LESSONS FOR THE REAL CHALLENGES OF INTERNATIONAL BUSINESS

RON CRUSE

iUniverse, Inc.
New York   Bloomington

LIES, BRIBES & PERIL

LESSONS FOR THE REAL CHALLENGES OF INTERNATIONAL BUSINESS

iUniverse books may be ordered through booksellers or by contacting:

iUniverse
1663 Liberty Drive
Bloomington, IN 47403
www.iuniverse.com
1-800-Authors (1-800-288-4677)

Because of the dynamic nature of the Internet, any Web addresses or links contained in this book may have changed since publication and may no longer be valid.

The views expressed in this work are solely those of the author and do not necessarily reflect the views of the publisher, and the publisher hereby disclaims any responsibility for them.

ISBN: 978-0-595-40678-4 (pbk)
ISBN: 978-0-595-85042-6 (ebk)

Printed in the United States of America
iUniverse rev. date: 03/11/2009

To
Bo, Sam, and Jack, for their inspiration and love.

In memory of
Sergey and William, whose friendship
and counsel remain lasting treasures.

Contents

Prologue

A heavily armed Apache helicopter swooped low to guard the perimeter of the Al Kut airfield. The sophisticated war machine's array of weaponry protruded menacingly from its armored fuselage creating, from my close proximity, an awe-inspiring vision. In May 2003, just weeks after the declared end of the Iraq War, the immediate area of Al Kut was assumed to be comparatively safe. The Apache's ominous presence made it clear the United States military was taking no chances. For the roughly two hours I was there, the Apache continued its circular vigil of the airfield, no more than thirty feet off the ground.

The aircraft hangar I was waiting in was haphazardly filled with huge pallets of meals ready to eat (MREs), water, and spare vehicle parts. It didn't appear too badly damaged by the very recent military battles. The same could not be said for the few Iraqi military vehicles within eyesight. Two large trucks had been destroyed by ordnance like a rocket-propelled grenade (RPG) or missile, and another was riddled by large bullet holes, probably from fifty-caliber machine-gun fire.

The visual references of the circling Apache and the war-ravaged vehicles lent a distinct air of danger to the site. Despite the relatively peaceful setting, a tension was palpable.

Milling about the hangar, oblivious to any threat of attack, were approximately thirty Army and Marine personnel. Some of them were busy but most were waiting just as aimlessly as I. My summary observation was that the Al Kut airfield and hangar were being used as a supply center and personnel transport hub to and from the war zone.

My wait was for a U.S. Marine CH-29 transport helicopter that was to fly me approximately sixty miles due east where the Expeditionary Force Headquarters was bivouacked in Al Hillah, Iraq. There, not more than a stone's throw from one of the Seven Wonders of the World—the ruins of the Hanging Gardens of Babylon—I was to meet with roughly twenty other U.S. contractors and a few of the highest ranking Coalition Forces officers to discuss the reconstruction of Iraq.

The risk of danger was not the issue keeping me and practically everyone else within the confines of the hangar. No, the overriding reason was that the sun felt like it was about five feet away. The temperature in the shade of the hangar was uncomfortable, but, out in the sun, it was unbearable. Temperatures in June often climb well over 120 degrees in Iraq.

Growing impatient with waiting and almost dizzy from watching the Apache circle and circle, I made my way over to one of the huge stacks of MREs near the mammoth opening of the hangar. There, perched casually against one side of the stack, an Army major was also quietly surveying the scene outside the hangar. Endeavoring to find a way to make time pass a bit more quickly, I struck up a conversation with the officer.

The major was a tall, thirtyish man with reddish brown hair, very well spoken and polite. He was an Army Intelligence officer and was rotating back to Kuwait for a few weeks before returning to Iraq. I didn't get that many specifics, but I gathered as our conversation continued that he had been with the main ground invasion force that had taken control of this east central region of Iraq.

As the conversation warmed, the major explained his duties in the days and weeks after the main invasion. Primarily those duties had consisted of intelligence gathering regarding the splinters of organized resistance that had remained. Also, and to a greater degree than expected, his duties had included dealing with the rampant crime that had broken out all over Iraq.

The major had been forced to deal with the problems associated with Saddam Hussein's release of almost one hundred thousand of Iraq's worst criminals in the days just before the war and with the harsh cultural realities that accompanied the problems. His reflections on the resulting cultural dilemmas he and the rest of the Coalition Forces faced were astute and perceptive.

While the Coalition Forces were focused on finding and eliminating organized resistance, the criminal element had taken up more and more attention in the days after the war. In general terms, when criminals were caught stealing or pillaging, they were interred for a few weeks or months, depending upon the crime. The major wryly explained there was no official infrastructure remaining in the country to judge or sentence criminals and that the whole process was mired in political sensibilities. These shortcomings created severe obstacles to the rehabilitation options available, but the real issue—the cultural chasm—resulted from the concept of punishment. To a resilient group of criminals normally expecting to have their ears and hands lopped off, or to be blinded by a hot poker, internment by the Coalition Forces came to be viewed as a holiday. In fact, many of the petty thieves came to know their captors well and even shared personal information. Clearly, the concept of confinement presenting a deterrent was a joke.

As I pondered the major's story, the image that came to mind was an Iraqi version of *Hogan's Heroes*, the old television comedy about allied officers detained in a World War II German prison camp. Apparently the Coalition Forces were viewed with the same level of trepidation by their Iraqi prisoners as Hogan and his men held for their primary captors, Colonel Klink and Sergeant Shultz—which was to say none at all.

As a businessman who had experienced many similar cultural paradoxes, I was not surprised. Indeed, Iraq was providing another confirmation of the tough practical lessons I had learned and that guided me in my global business travels.

Over the coming months, as the insurgency intensified, a direct consequence of this cultural deterrent chasm became the largest scandal of the Iraqi conflict—Abu Ghraib. There's no doubt in my mind the misdeeds at that prison escalated out of the frustration borne from the real life *Hogan's Heroes* situations presented when dealing with Iraqi criminals. Perhaps nothing could have prevented the misguided actions at Abu Ghraib, but maybe, just maybe, a more enlightened understanding by the Coalition Forces of cultural chasms, and the often resultant pitfalls, could have helped to assuage the frustration and thus prevented that terrible scandal.

By chronicling and attempting to lend some understanding to cultural disparities like those faced by the Coalition Forces, my book will offer some practical solutions to the cultural challenges that can seem so complex and can make doing business worldwide so daunting. The lessons I have learned over my twenty-five years of globetrotting are not to be found in college or business schools, yet they can help serve as an indispensable guide to success. And, I believe, these lessons are as critical for the soldiers patrolling the streets of Baghdad as they are for the businesspeople selling computers in Europe, medical supplies in Asia, or jeep parts in war-torn regions. In today's often shifty, usually fickle, corporate environments, these simple lessons can also pay big dividends right here in the United States.

As I fled the specter of hungry lions in Kenya, dodged bullets in Pakistan, faced Mafia-type confrontation in Kazakhstan, dealt with the repercussions of the murder of a Russian joint venture partner, or scrambled to escape various countries boiling with civil unrest, I realized that understanding culture is elemental to business. Native culture affects perceptions, actions, logic, legal frameworks, and even danger.

Against the backdrop of building three international businesses, I will demonstrate how my lessons in culture, with the intrinsic components of logic and saving face, along with the directly related lessons of communications, accommodation, negotiation, and jurisprudence, can be instrumental to understanding, and hence successfully conducting, business throughout today's very perilous and risky world. Also, lessons in problem solving and the practicalities of international travel demonstrate how critical the application of simple rules can be to success. Lastly, I hope to establish how essential developing and trusting intuition can be to business achievement. I believe it will be evident that the application of these lessons can be the difference between sweet success and bitter failure.

To appreciate how I got to Iraq, how my lessons were garnered and formed, and how important they have been to my career, I need to start at the beginning of my adventures. The beginning of my career in "the mud," that is the "Third World" or "developing nations," as political correctness came to dictate they be called, began in the sands of the Arabian Peninsula in the early 1980s. My journey would take me from Saudi Arabia across the Middle East, throughout Africa and Asia, into Russia and the new republics formed after the fall of the former Soviet Union. Then, following the history-altering events of September 11, 2001, I would encounter some of the most extreme and dangerous situations of my career in the ancient lands of Afghanistan and Iraq.

During the initial stages of my career learning the "easy" way was certainly not my forte. In those days, I learned my lessons by what could definitely be termed the school of hard knocks and many of the knocks were so forceful that I coined them my "two-by-four" learning system. Basically, my lessons were learned as if I'd suffered blunt force trauma from a two-by-four piece of lumber. Usually, the psychological wounds developed into lessons learned that became indispensable tools on the road to success. The continual encounters with lies, bribes, and peril presented regular blows of varying degrees of anguish and often a bit of humor.

In the beginning, I didn't have a clue—not even close to a clue—but I knew if I was to be successful, I had better get one.

Arabian Daze:
An Introductory Lesson
on the Importance of Culture

The crowded terminal resembled nothing so much as the bar scene from the original *Star Wars* motion picture, where no two creatures were alike.

There were Hajiis, Muslims on pilgrimage to Mecca, draped in terrycloth, which was all they wore. Throughout the crowd was a sprinkling of Tibetan monks in orange wraps. There were Nigerians and other West Africans in bright tribal robes, along with Ethiopians and Eritreans in even more colorful garb. I could see the stocky Hutus and tall Tutsis from Rwanda and Burundi. There were Zulus from South Africa and the hunting people from Kenya and Tanganyika, the Masai. I saw Indians and Pakistanis in classic Nehru attire and other Asians dressed in various traditional clothing. And, as expected, there were Saudis with their full-body thobes and head scarves, or *ghutter*. Saudis abhorred physical labor. Their immigrant workforce, recruited from all over the world, was represented there in the terminal.

It was 1982 and my first overseas business trip. I was twenty-six years old and had been recently promoted and transferred from New York to Los Angeles to head the company's biggest commercial contract. I had absolutely no idea what to expect in the coming minutes let alone the two weeks ahead of me.

Ostensibly, I was traveling to meet a company-chartered Boeing 747. It was filled with approximately twenty million dollars in supplies bound for hospitals near the top of the 8,500-foot Azir Mountain Range just southeast of Jeddah. As the wheels of the jet I had boarded in London touched down on the runway in Jeddah, I looked forward to the days ahead, but not without apprehension.

We taxied to the tarmac jetway. I collected my carry-on bags and then walked from the aircraft into a surreal scene I will never forget. It was two o'clock in the morning, yet hundreds of massed travelers packed the new, ornate terminal to overflowing. I had never seen anything like it.

The visual clash of this magnificent modern airport facility with this varied, multi-robed, often bedraggled worker force was striking. It seemed to me that every hired hand was in Jeddah that night, right there in the transit lounge. Surprisingly, for such a large group, it was unusually quiet.

My nose was also sending new signals to my brain. As stuffy as I was from the long flight, I could distinctly smell the rich combination of a crowded high school gymnasium intermixed with sweaty socks—really sweaty socks—wafting from the crowd. The air was also permeated with various odors of exotic tobacco. Whiffs of the smoke carried a very sharp, acrid smell coming from cheap hand-rolled cigarettes. Interspersed with it was the pungent sweet aroma of the clove cigarettes favored by Indonesians. The smoke hung over the throng in a pungent blue cloud.

As I looked closer, it seemed to me that the mass collectively possessed every attribute and affliction of the human condition. Badly decayed teeth, defective eyes, and skin ailments were universal. No, Toto, this certainly wasn't Kansas.

As if all this wasn't sensory overload enough, a question formed in my jet lag–fogged brain as to why the terminal was so damn crowded in the middle of the night. London Heathrow, where I'd transited, was the busiest airport in the world and was all but deserted at this time of night. Later that week, I learned that the daylight desert air became so hot that it produced insufficient lift for the long-haul flights to and from Europe and Asia.

Stepping off the airplane, I might have thought I was prepared for a brave new world of sights and experiences, but within minutes, I realized that was not the case. I was immediately developing a healthy appreciation for the cultural dichotomy into which I was now stepping, one that would both befuddle and bedazzle me over the next two decades.

While I was dealing with the sensory overload, the airport paging system suddenly emitted a loud wailing sound. I would have guessed the heterogeneous mass had almost nothing in common yet over half of them began dropping to their knees and small carpets appeared out of nowhere. *This must be prayer time*, I realized. I had seen the ritual in news reports and knew little more than the fact that it was a Muslim religious rite.

Had I been magically placed in a real incarnation of the *Star Wars* bar scene, I would have felt no more out of place. I stood there in the lounge, just stunned at the sight spread before me and wondered for a panicked second what the heck I was doing there.

As the mass of humanity prepared for prayer, I was hit by a call to nature. I elbowed my way around the standing non-Muslims to a men's room adjacent to the transit lounge. Since Jeddah was a major Red Sea port on the western shore of the Arabian Peninsula, and its new airport was built to swank Western specifications, I entered the restroom with very Western expectations. I should have known better.

The first thing I spotted was a Bedouin sitting on one sink with his feet in another, both faucets at full blast, happily washing his ankles and toes. I resorted to my New York acquired subway "cool" and tried to appear as nonchalant as possible. It wasn't easy as water was splashing everywhere. Casually giving him a wide a berth, I made my way to a urinal.

Standing there, I sensed something more was going on. Unconscious of why, I looked *up* to my left and locked eyes with a face, the head wrapped in what looked to be a bright red and white towel, positioned well above the seven-foot-high toilet stalls. This Bedouin had a very matter-of-fact demeanor, as if it was normal for him to be occupying that vantage point, looking down on the row of urinals with his head just centimeters from the ceiling.

My sense of the normal was now completely gone. As the noises and odors from the man's stall made it very clear what was going on—he was standing on the toilet as he used it—I tried to glance away, feigning indifference. If ever in my life I looked like a deer caught in the headlights, it was right at that moment.

As my travels increased in that area of the world, I learned that the scene in the Jeddah airport bathroom was quite normal and based on a major tenet of Islam: ritualistic cleansing before prayer. These ablutions, or *wudhu*, included the washing of hands, mouth, inside and outside the nose, the face, forearms, neck, ears, and finally the feet and ankles. The rules require that each must be washed three times prior to prayer.

Complicating the prayer ritual even further, Islam lays out events that break the wudhu. These include answering calls of nature, sleeping while leaning against a support, injury, drawing blood, or vomiting. If any of these happen, the entire process has to be repeated. My buddy with the lofty vantage point was making certain there would be no call of nature once he'd started his ablutions. My guess was that's where the guy washing his feet in the sink had been moments before I entered the restroom. They were both preparing for prayer.

I returned to the multitude to get a boarding pass for my connecting flight to Dhahran, located two hours directly east on the Persian Gulf. It had not been possible to order a boarding pass in advance for the flights, so I had to figure out the process upon arrival in Jeddah. Every arriving passenger with another destination within Saudi Arabia also had to obtain a pass, so I assumed it would be a well-established and straightforward proposition. I couldn't have been more wrong.

Looking about me, I could see no logic or order to the scene. I had absolutely no idea how to get the boarding pass, and I didn't have a lot of time. Searching for some sign of where to go and what to do next, I was slowly gripped with quiet panic.

After several minutes, I spotted a sign written in English indicating a transit service desk. But there was also a mob crushed against the counter. Behind me, a sardonic Brit caught my expression and increasing anxiety. "You know, they don't queue up over here," he said helpfully. I nodded my head in thanks, as if I understood him. *Queue? Oh yes, line. They don't line up here. No line?* I thought. *How the hell am I supposed to get to the counter?*

I watched the drill unfolding in front of me. There were at least a hundred hands in the air and the clamor for help was in a dozen tongues and accents. Everyone was shouting *"Shoof,"* which someone told me was Arabic for "Look!" so I joined in. At the time, my reaction was more instinctive than reasoned, but it was correct. As the old adage goes, when in Rome…

I held my papers and passport in both hands, waded into the melee, and, while applying a bit of forward pressure, found myself slowly inching toward the desk. After a prolonged and crowded wait, my passport and a boarding pass were handed back over the gaggle of wrapped heads. When I finally boarded my plane, I was exhausted.

To say that I had run a gamut of unfamiliar experiences would be an understatement. From the incredible sounds and sights of the arrivals hall, the mass prayer scene, and from the inexplicable confrontations in the bathroom to the wild scene at the transit desk, I was broadsided into a stunned realization that my trip to that point had not evolved quite as I had expected. As the plane took off toward Dhahran, I grappled with my first lesson in cultural differences.

I landed in Dhahran at daybreak. The terminal there was shabby compared to Jeddah and every bit as disorganized. I emerged from the air-conditioned building into the open air feeling for an instant as if I'd walked into a solid wall of heat and humidity. It's so muggy on the Persian Gulf that walking is like wading through water. The 98 percent humidity and ninety-degree temperature at six o'clock in the morning intermixed with my jet lag and fatigue to overwhelm me. In that drained condition, I unthinkingly flagged the first cab I spotted. The ten-minute ride to my hotel scarcely left me time to compute the ratio of *riyals* to dollars. When the courteous driver asked for two hundred *riyals*, or sixty dollars, for a thirty-*riyal* ride, I simply paid.

As the cab sped away, I experienced a very mild, nearly imperceptible, sense of loss. But in my state I couldn't place the feeling precisely. It was only as I checked into the hotel that I had realized what had happened. *You just got screwed*, I thought as I signed the registration card. I had learned that I needed to be more careful, but the recognition of the real lesson, learning to understand and trust my intuition, would come later.

All in all, my learning experience in the taxi came cheap compared to others. It had cost just over fifty dollars. Some of my later lessons would occur with millions of dollars at stake.

Cultural Snapshot

Most toilets in the Middle East are an open hole, and the locals just hike up their robes, or *thobes*, when they use them. After my experience in the Jeddah airport, I understood why the lavatory seats on planes and in terminals throughout the Middle East are always cracked and often completely broken. In the years to come, the unusual banging and rustling coming from airplane lavatories in this part of the world would not puzzle me in the least. Imagine trying to stand on an airplane toilet dressed in a robe!

Mohammed's Muse:
A Lesson in Communication

A quick bit of background at this point should suffice to give an idea of how I had arrived at this point in my life. My father, a World War II combat veteran, was an educational psychologist and civilian employee of the U.S. Army. I was born near Ft. Sill, Oklahoma, where he worked. My mom was a Scotswoman and war bride. Her father had been with the British Colonies Office, and, from an early age, she regaled me with exciting stories of their travels and adventures in the exotic lands that remained colonies of the crown. Mom had a real estate license and later became a public accountant. I believe it was from her I acquired my entrepreneurial spirit as well as my wanderlust. From my father I inherited an intrinsic sense of value and an attitude predisposed, as I had it force-fed most of my childhood, to do things "right"—a mixture of values I would come to find not all that common in the business world.

Officially, I studied economics and sociology at Villanova University, getting a first class education. But, I primarily devoted myself to organizing the Delta Tau Delta fraternity parties. I learned more about business, essentially the art of making money, from them than I ever did in any classroom or from any book. The decision to go to New York City after graduation was pivotal to my life and career, so like most young men I made it for a compelling reason—I was dating a girl who lived there. I soon landed a spot at a Wall Street brokerage selling municipal bonds and then worked for a time pushing wholesale bonds, hating both jobs.

To be honest, I wasn't that great of an employee. The reality was that I was pitifully unprepared for the business world. Years later, I became my own measure of the total lack of responsible thought in young men in their early twenties. Whenever I'm contemplating the hire of some bright, shining star with a new diploma, I often make the decision by comparing him to myself at the same age. If he's no worse than I was, I hire him. I say "him" because women, from my experience, do not suffer this particular malaise to the degree or for the duration of their male counterparts.

Fed up with my work on Wall Street, I finally met with a headhunter who referred me to Four Winds International, a shipping firm specializing in international freight forwarding.

In many ways, it was a perfect fit. Before long I became the leading salesperson in the firm's six U.S. offices, as well as manager of the New York office. I was maturing on the low end of the guy maturity scale. Nevertheless, I was slowly beginning to have serious, responsible thoughts on an almost daily basis. When I was offered a director-level position in Los Angeles, and, with it, the chance to become the youngest senior executive in the company, I accepted. I had just turned twenty-six, the age at which guys either begin to have thoughts other than about girls and partying, or they never do. Luckily, I had found a vocation I enjoyed. I was determined to be good at it, yet I was not sure what skills I would need to develop to succeed. My first overseas assignment was the trip to Saudi Arabia to meet the 747 charter plane with the $20 million in medical supplies and learn what the heck was going on there.

It quickly became apparent that new skills were mandatory if I was to enjoy any measure of success.

After the fleecing by the taxi driver accompanying the arrival to my hotel in Dhahran, I took a brief nap then attempted a simply awful breakfast that included powdered milk, something akin to putting Coffee-mate® in water. Then I went to the company's local office, a small, shabby building made of concrete with an air conditioner so loud you had to shout to be heard over it. It was the same everywhere for the days I was there. I had to raise my voice in every office I visited just to make myself heard.

My main obligation on this first trip was to meet that 747 charter flight that was arriving in Taif, just southeast of Jeddah. The trip to Dhahran had been planned as a way to kill time prior to that charter flight arrival and also to allow me to gain valuable exposure to this part of the world. The latter purpose was certainly achieved in spades. So, I flew back to Jeddah where I was met by Mohammed, whom we called Uncle Mo, the local Saudi agent, and by Rod, the American office manager.

Rod was a former U.S. Navy Seal with a lingering military demeanor. He was tall, perhaps thirty years old, and well built. Uncle Mo was a stereotypical Saudi with olive skin and dark hair. He had a huge hooked nose and a mole the size of a nickel exactly between his eyes. He was tall for a Saudi, though a bit chubby, and wore the traditional *thobe* and *ghutra*. Like most Saudis, he exuded a confident attitude that completely belied the haphazard manner in which all events were handled.

After exchanging greetings, Uncle Mo informed me that we would meet with clients the following day. The first of these meetings was to be my initial encounter with a Saudi client. I don't remember what my expectations were exactly, but, based on what I'd seen so far, I believed I was ready for anything, which only shows how little I knew. Despite my attitude, that first meeting was a real awakening to international business practices in general and Saudi business practices specifically.

At the meeting, I was introduced by Uncle Mo as we sat down. Immediately, Uncle Mo and the client switched from English and conducted the rest of the conversation entirely in Arabic. Although Uncle Mo sporadically uttered a guttural aside in English to me, I had absolutely no idea what was transpiring. I tried to nod and appear involved whenever they either gestured my way or looked to me. For all I knew, they could have been discussing just how stupid Americans were, and I could have been agreeing with them.

To add to my sense of the surreal, midway through the meeting, a group of Saudi businessmen was escorted into the room, yet no introductions were made. Once in the office, these newcomers were quite attentive to whatever Uncle Mo was saying. I didn't know why they were there, but I assumed I should nod occasionally in their direction as well.

Leaving the room after bidding smiling good-byes, Uncle Mo leaned over and said, "That was a very good meeting, Ron." I asked him what had been said, and he responded with a shrug allowing that everything had gone very well, yes, very well indeed. I was not happy about being in the dark during the meeting, but the most puzzling aspect was the attendance of the other businessmen. I questioned Uncle Mo regarding the other people who had been ushered into the room.

Uncle Mo cavalierly explained that they were scheduled for the next meeting with our client. In Saudi Arabia, business courtesies meant being allowed into the office early, since leaving people to "cool their heels" was considered an insult. If my inbound flight and surreal airport experiences had not fully prepared me, I belatedly realized that the cultural peculiarities I had witnessed also extended to business practices. Suddenly, I really felt foolish. Those other guys must have thought I had something wrong with my head—some kind of involuntary tic. I had nodded at them at least a dozen times after their entrance.

I was not happy. I realized I not only didn't know *exactly* what had transpired but, to be frank, I had no idea even *generally* what had happened. It was pretty damn clear to me that I better make sure that kind of situation never occurred again. I also decided to remove constant nodding from my meeting gestures.

Over the next few years, I learned such cultural differences were the norm rather than the exception in all eighty countries in which I conducted business.

This initial experience with an interpreter, if what Uncle Mo had done could be properly considered as such, constituted a valuable lesson in communication. From that moment on, encompassing almost twenty years and hundreds of meetings overseas, I insisted that all meetings be simultaneously translated.

Cultural Snapshot

The contrast between the desert outside and the interior of buildings was figuratively day and night. Exterior temperatures hovered well over 110 degrees, though the inside of a car after sitting in the sun was more like 140. To battle the insufferable heat, offices and residences were air conditioned well below 70 degrees, which meant I was always either boiling or freezing.

The car ride experiences were no less perplexing than the ones in the Jeddah airport. Old dirt roads, that became all but impassably muddy on the rare occasions when rain fell, led to six-lane concrete superhighways going nowhere. The superhighways would suddenly end without warnings or markers, usually giving way to a three or four-foot drop back down to an ancient dirt road.

A Yodeling Custom:
A Lesson in Accommodation

The next morning the charter of medical supplies was due to land. In typical Saudi fashion, Uncle Mo had decided that he must have a new car. Uncle Mo wanted to buy the car *now*, so that's what he was doing. Like many people and all children under the age of five, delayed gratification was not something he had mastered.

Rod and I learned of the diversion when we went to the office to meet him. We were told Uncle Mo was not there but that he had gone to the local Chevrolet dealer. American cars were all the rage in this hot, desert country, as the Europeans had not yet rivaled the Americans' manufacture of decent auto air conditioners.

Rod and I arrived at the car dealership, which quite surreally looked just like a typical dealership in the United States, only set in the middle of the desert. There was Uncle Mo in the service area, standing in ankle deep water, his *thobe* hiked up over his knees, overseeing the washing of his new Chevy. With the charter due on the ground in less than an hour and the airport at least an hour's drive away, I couldn't believe what was transpiring. Rod was angry, but he didn't seem surprised. The day before, Mo had assured us repeatedly that he understood how important this flight was and that there would be "mafi mushkila" *no problem*, the ever-feared retort.

Rod and I had to shout over the spraying water and other machinery in the service area to be heard. We begged Uncle Mo to go with us immediately, but he was like a child with a new toy, laughing and splashing in the water, dreamily watching the sun flash off the chrome on his brand new automobile. It was just all too ridiculous. Rod screamed something unintelligible to Uncle Mo and waved for me to go. We jumped in the car and headed off. It was no wonder things were such a mess in this country.

Rod and I drove to Taif, a relatively cool mountain city located some four thousand feet above sea level. There the airport had runways long enough to handle big jets, built to accommodate the king's fleet, since the royal family made Taif its summer residence. It was in Taif that our chartered 747 was due.

The primary reason our charter was landing in Taif was because a small portion of what we were importing, such as cough syrup, was technically illegal because it contained alcohol. Uncle Mo was from the area, and his cousin was the head customs officer, which should have been a most favorable situation for us. Thinking about Uncle Mo splashing in the water with his new car with a complete disregard for the time, I was beginning to have my doubts.

When Rod and I arrived at the airport, we immediately went inside the terminal. We were an hour late. The reality was that without our Saudi agent, Uncle Mo, there was nothing to be done. For reasons that escape me now and that defied my most immediate experiences, I expected to find an orderly bureaucratic process at the airport in Taif. I was totally unprepared for the reality.

The arriving goods were actually the property of the Saudi government. No shipment should have been more routine or more easily sanctioned than a Saudi government shipment for a Saudi government hospital. Here, as I would find so often, the left hand of the Saudi government was importing the supplies, while the right hand of the Saudi government was creating obstacles that prevented the supplies from entering.

When Uncle Mo arrived at the airport some two hours later, Rod and I were fit to be tied. The 747 had been on the ground for nearly three hours, but Mo appeared undisturbed by our agitation. He greeted his cousin and kissed him on both cheeks in the manner of Arab males.

Uncle Mo's cousin, whose name I never caught, was the ideal head customs officer. He was both deaf and mute. He was also a stereotypical Arab in appearance though a lot chubbier than most. His *thobe* was two or three sizes too small, and conspicuously short.

Although aware the cousin was mute, when he first warbled to communicate I was a bit astonished. His vocal intonations were a bubbling sing-song to which Uncle Mo smiled, nodded his head, and yodeled in reply, apparently an aural vibration that the deaf cousin understood quite well. He and Uncle Mo, carrying a sack of Saudi currency, then headed out the door toward the customs area with me dutifully in tow.

They entered a small, partially air-conditioned customs shed, pointedly leaving me outside. Even though we were at altitude, it was still hot as hell in the sun. So, I sought shelter along the shade line of the small building. I could hear the cousin's chirping and Uncle Mo's yodeling through the thin walls but had no understanding of what was taking place

The pair came out in less than twenty minutes. Not surprisingly, Uncle Mo's sack had vanished. Everything was cleared through customs. Once the supplies were off the plane, we trucked them fifty miles up the escarpment, another two thousand feet above sea level, to the hospital.

I was aware the bag of cash had played a major role in the clearance, but I wasn't completely sure in what context. I hated to think it was bribery, so I chose to believe it was what I came to call accommodation.

Accommodation is a worldwide practice that can manifest in very diverse and subtle forms, and no concept, cultural or otherwise, is more misunderstood by Americans. While many might think accommodation is nothing more than a classic case of bribery, they are wrong. That word is much too harsh, with too many negative connotations to describe the intricate process. Accommodation constitutes the very basis of interaction in the business world and is the elemental quid pro quo, *this for that*, that is the foundation of business. The problem with accommodation as practiced in most of the world, Europe certainly not excluded, is that the custom is the close cousin of corruption.

The Egyptian Trader:
A Lesson in Negotiation

Continuing on that first memorable journey in 1982, I flew on to Egypt. Cairo's old airport had the look of an old railroad station and presented a scene that could have come right out of an Indiana Jones movie. The huge flights signboard announcing the departing and arriving flights had most letters missing from it. Reading the sign was like figuring a crossword puzzle.

As I entered the cryptlike terminal, I encountered Egyptian immigration. Their method for clearing passports was all but incomprehensible. I really thought that, I was prepared for just about anything. Yet, I never could have conjured up anything so inefficient and chaotic.

The archaic system used sloping boards, ostensibly to aid in moving passports. In actuality, the "system" served to jumble them all up in a disorganized mélange. Each time passports were moved they became more and more hopelessly disorganized, and I watched my own passport vanish somewhere into the mess. I waited and waited for almost two hours. At one point, I nonchalantly peered into an empty office and eyed a four-foot high growing mountain of passports.

Finally, I appealed to a very nice Egyptian lady. She disappeared and returned with some fifty U.S. passports. I assume she dug through the pile to find them. She meticulously opened each one, looking at the passport picture and then back at me. This went on for some time until I matched a picture. With a curt smile, she stamped a page and handed my passport over.

Exiting the terminal, I was immediately besieged by aggressive beggars. Outside, in the dirt and heat, my first impression was of abject poverty. People shoved at me from all sides, shouting "Baksheesh," a term infamous worldwide for its payoff and bribery connotations. I saw young mothers with infants and white-eyed beggars with cups. Such total cataracts are common in Egypt because of the incessant exposure to the desert sun. There is nothing spookier than to look at someone and see only white in their eyes.

I stayed at the Nile Hilton, sited just yards from the exotic Nile River. Entering my air-conditioned room, I looked out of the window across the expanse of historic water and thought of all the trading that had taken place along those banks since ancient times. Throughout the city were the world famous *souks* and *khans*. History suggests otherwise, but local legend has it that Marco Polo traded in these same marketplaces.

One of the by-products of traveling internationally was learning to fill periods of mind-numbingly boring downtime. It is often impossible to schedule flights and meetings into a neatly compressed timeframe. In Egypt, as well as Saudi Arabia and later in Pakistan, I spent that downtime in the marketplaces, *khans*, and carpet *souks*.

In these marketplaces of the Middle East, and from the merchants who had been plying their trades in the same fashion for centuries, I learned the basics of the art of negotiation.

For the uninitiated, buying merchandise in the *souks* of the Middle East is more aptly described as haggling warfare than as shopping. In the Middle East, as with most places in the mud, there is no such thing as a fixed price—everything is negotiable. If you don't learn the basics of haggling, you will forever be paying too much.

The crux of all negotiation lies in the fact that the seller wants to make the maximum money possible, and the buyer wants to pay the minimum price—it's axiomatic. I was about to learn how to bridge that chasm.

Prior to my first visit to the Khan el Khalili, the teeming ancient market in Cairo where one might imagine actually bumping into Marco Polo, or at least his ghost, I was warned of the haggling ways of the merchants. Khan el Khalili, founded by the Emir Djaharks el-Khalili in 1382, is perhaps the oldest market in the world. Such was the success of the Khan in the fifteenth century that some claim it was responsible for Christopher Columbus's search for alternate routes from the East and hence the discovery of the New World.

The market area was a maze of narrow stone passageways snaking between shops crammed to overflowing with their offerings. The centuries of foot traffic and the history oozing from every nook of the Khan were brought into sharp focus from the trails worn unevenly into the primeval stone passageways.

I had been warned by Lynn, the wife of my company's American manager there in Cairo, to never accept the first price advanced by any merchant. I was advised to actually leave the shop and return later with a lower offer. Damn if I understood the tactic, but I decided to try it.

I found a carpet I liked in one of the overstuffed souks and asked the merchant, to my mind's eye a reincarnation of Emir Djaharks, the price. He gave me a price for the carpet that seemed high. Following the instructions I had received, I shook my head no and promptly exited the souk. After weaving my way through some other shops and finding nothing to my liking, I returned to the carpet souk.

Emir met me as I entered, and I promptly informed him I would pay him half of his price for the carpet. Emir countered with a price in between, and I again left the souk. After a short while, I returned. Emir and I had a similar conversation. Again, I left after no mutually agreeable price was achieved. Disappointed, I returned to my hotel.

Relating my carpet souk experience over dinner that evening I received an additional tip. Lynn suggested I take a taxi back to Khan el Khalili early the next morning and be Emir's very first customer of the day. She explained that a local superstition dictated that it was good luck to make a sale to the first customer of the day.

Following Lynn's advice I arose early and arrived at Khalili just as many of the shops were opening. Weaving my way deep into the maze, I found Emir's carpet souk just as he opened. Emir greeted me warmly and offered me chai, the over-sweetened tea so popular in that region of the world.

While we sipped chai together, I made Emir another offer, and again he countered. I turned to leave the shop, and, as I did, he finally relented. "Mafi mushkila," he said. *No problem.* "We have a deal." Taking the agreed upon price in Egyptian pounds, Emir explained he would have good luck the remainder of the day. Damn if it didn't work. I walked away with the carpet, reveling in my victory.

What I had learned was the essence of negotiation. It's so simple. You must always know your leverage. Often, that leverage is nothing more than being willing to walk away from the deal as I had done in the carpet souk. And, of course, leverage is the bridge over the chasm.

I also became aware that leverage can take various forms. In the souks of the Middle East, one of those forms was a belief among the merchants that to make a sale to the first customer of the day is a harbinger of good luck. This added leverage was enough to achieve the right price. As time went on, I realized these simple rules could be used in any negotiating context, although one must know and understand the local cultural forms of leverage.

Knowing the simple rules of negotiating, being ready at all times to walk away, and watching carefully for any opportunities to increase my leverage served me very well over the coming years.

Cultural Snapshot

The city of Cairo remained one of my very favorite destinations, even though the rising tide of Islamic fundamentalism visibly entrenched itself in Egypt. I was in and out of Cairo over twenty times in the next dozen years. With each subsequent visit, I watched the stylish Western appearance of the local Egyptian women transformed to the black-covered abaya demanded by the fundamentalists. This change was a harbinger of the evolving cultural polarization between the Middle East and the West that would erupt twenty years later.

On one trip home, I remember a gorgeous sunset descent into the Rome airport that gave me a panoramic view of much of the Italian Peninsula. The sky was streaked with reds and purples. I thought it a splendid end to such a life-altering journey.

Omar's Dog Tale:
A Lesson in Cultural Sensitivity

The lesson that cultures are intrinsically different and hold profoundly different values was impressed on me again and again as my travels continued. As background to this affair, I was in Jeddah on one of my repeated trips and happened to notice a large number of stray dogs and inquired why this was. I learned that most Arabs regard dogs to be unclean and do not view them as objects of affection. Whether a dog was to live or die wouldn't matter in the least.

The basis for this, I was told, lay in the teachings of the Prophet, known as the Hadith. Many Muslims believe that an angel will not enter a room if a dog is present, so the conclusion is that dogs must be bad. I was also told that the Hadith teaches that anything a dog touches must be washed seven times, the final ablution being in dust. Heck, I'm not even sure how to go about the last part, so it's no small wonder most Muslims avoid dogs as if they were the plague.

On these trips to Saudi Arabia, I came to know Omar, a tall Sudanese with a beaming smile and enormous Afro. He worked in the Jeddah office there along with Rod and a fellow named Lee. Lee was the epitome of the vagabond adventurer, someone I would share some remarkable experiences with over the coming years. Relatively short and dark-haired, he was one of the most naturally funny people I've ever known.

Omar was especially eager to improve his English and knowledge of all things American. His enthusiasm for almost all Western habits stopped—understandably in light of his religious teachings—well short of any affection for dogs. Culturally, he was *incapable* of understanding that other people might have different feelings about dogs. This is ethnocentricity in the extreme, but it is more common than you might think. A real predicament arose from this simple cultural belief.

One day, an American oil executive arrived in the Kingdom accompanied by his wife. I'll call them the Joneses. They were going to be living in a specially built, corporate compound near Yanbo, a refining city located north of

Jeddah. Mrs. Jones wanted this to be as normal an experience as possible, so they had decided to bring their family dog, a terrier named Little Muffy.

Mrs. Jones wanted Little Muffy shipped into the Kingdom from the United States, so we offered to lend assistance. It was Omar's responsibility for clearing shipments through Saudi customs so Lee explained to Omar that he was to make it his mission to quickly clear the dog through customs so no ill fortune could befall it. That was top priority. "I understand," Omar said solemnly. "I've looked into it. It is absolutely possible. We will do this together." Nice words, but Omar, as it became quite apparent later, viewed Little Muffy as nothing more than another piece of freight.

The day arrived, and Omar and Lee went to the airport. The Joneses eagerly awaited their pet's arrival outside the customs area. Inside the baggage claim area, Omar was being dutiful and stood watching as a dog cage came around on the luggage conveyor. Lee picked up the cage, which was ominously quiet. Opening the latch, the men peered in and discovered that the terrier had succumbed to the rigors of the flight, apparently suffering a horrible death. Little Muffy's paws were spread grotesquely, its graying tongue was hanging out, and his bloodshot eyes were wide open—all signs of acute oxygen deprivation.

Lee, aghast, tried to straighten the paws and close the terrier's eyes, desperately trying to make it seem as if the animal had died peacefully. Omar recoiled in disbelief that Lee would actually touch a dog, especially one that was so obviously dead.

"What are we going to say to Mr. and Mrs. Jones?" Lee said aloud. Omar was silent, probably trying to understand why this was a problem. Being very task-oriented, Omar picked up the cage and went to clear it through customs as instructed.

Lee could not bring himself to go outside the customs area to inform the family. Finally, he summoned the courage and walked out with Omar. They were a Mutt-and-Jeff team, Omar at six-feet-four inches in height, and Lee, five-foot-eight. Lee's face was grim while Omar was quite businesslike. He'd completed his job very efficiently.

The Joneses warmly greeted Lee and his companion. Lee lowered his eyes and pawed the ground with one foot, trying to find the appropriate words. Unfazed, Omar filled the awkward silence by declaring very matter-of-factly and unemotionally, "Mrs. Jones, your dog is *very* dead."

Lee, astonished, realized immediately that Omar had no understanding of the emotional currents in play over the deceased terrier. For Omar's part, he thought the stunned silence was due to concern over the difficult customs issues involving a dead dog. So, he added with a conspiratorial smile and wink, "But do not worry, I have cleared it through customs."

The silence was deafening. No words came to Lee, who, no doubt, wanted to shoot himself. Mrs. Jones, equally speechless, hovered on the edge of hysteria. Again, filling the sound vacuum, Omar boastfully added with pride, "It's a very big deal here to clear a dead dog. We should be congratulated!"

The Joneses, although deeply upset, understood that Muffy's death was a terrible accident. They had traveled enough to grasp the plethora of cultural landmines and to instinctively grasp the unintentional disdain displayed by Omar. Their international experience and understanding were the only reasons the consequences were not disastrous.

The story remained the subject of some humor, and Omar always behaved as if he understood, but he never really got it. From that time on—among the wide circle that came to hear the story—whenever bad news had to be relayed, someone would say with an Arabic accent, "Your dog is *very* dead."

To say Omar could not understand the emotional reaction of the Joneses' is an understatement. It was simply *culturally* beyond him. He meant well. He hadn't wanted to upset them. In truth, that would have been the very last thing the ever-affable Sudanese would mean to do. To his very soul he just couldn't relate to the Joneses emotional attachment to their pet dog. For him, the culture gap regarding dogs was an insurmountable chasm. The Muffy issue was forever emblazoned in my mind as the quintessential insight illuminating the unforeseen and inexplicable cultural issues that can arise in the normal course of business. You can't possibly know every cultural dilemma, but you need to appreciate the crazy, and often lethal, impact of them on business.

A Parisian, a Sudanese and a Bedouin: A Lesson in Cross-Cultural Communication

I returned to the mud later that year, stopping in Paris on my way. What took place was my first extended business exposure to people who can comfortably converse in several languages. Like most Americans, I knew one language and had never felt a need to learn another. After this trip, I never felt that way again.

What had impressed me was the fact that so many Europeans *can* speak two or more languages. The person who brought all this to my rapt attention was a young woman, cute, petite, dark-haired, and, best of all, named Gigi. What could be better for a young American guy's first tour of Paris and its intoxicating nightlife? She spoke four languages effortlessly, and I was smitten by her heavily accented English. She taught me how to order drinks like a Parisian, and I thought that life just couldn't get better. The entire evening was right out of the movies—the only thing missing was Maurice Chevalier.

During dinner with a Frenchman named Jean-Claude, a former racecar driver—every self-respecting Frenchman must have some devil-may-care background—and his associates, jokes were told around the table in no less than four languages. Occasionally, the translation from one language, whether French, Italian, or German, to English just didn't make sense. Gigi tried to help me share the humor, but often it just wouldn't convey. Occasionally, the others would roar as a joke was told in German or Italian, only for all to agree it wasn't funny in the least when relayed to me in English. I have never felt as inferior as I did that night, trapped in my monolinguistic world. It was clear that ineffective communication can cause problems, even in a casual social setting where millions of dollars are not at stake.

Occurring in the proximate time frame were two incidents involving Lee, one with him as the seeming culprit and another where he was the foil. Both portray insights on cross-language communications.

Lee took great pleasure in exposing real cultural dilemmas. He quickly caught on to the fact that language—communications if you will—was a veritable bottomless well of opportunities. If one wants to explore the sensitivities surrounding cultural differences, delving into any sexual connotation usually provides ample territory. Omar, always eager to learn and to use American "cool" slang, was one of Lee's favorite targets. His truly devoted Muslim upbringing and his desire to be cool made for some humorous situations.

At Omar's constant prodding, Lee taught Omar quite a lexicon of various inappropriate American slang words. When Omar learned that the informal first name of Four Winds' boss of bosses was one of these inappropriate slang words and that he was commonly called this name to his face, Omar could not believe it. He thought it was another of Lee's practical jokes.

During one of my visits, Omar pulled me aside and asked under his breath if people indeed called the Big Boss "Dick" to his face. I grinned, instantly realizing Omar's quandary, and told him that yes, in fact, everyone did. The look of anguish on Omar's face was priceless. It was just culturally more than he could take. In Arabic, the corresponding slang word was rarely spoken and then only in hushed terms. It was *unfathomable* to Omar that a word such as this could be used as a name.

Not long after that conversation with Omar, I was with Lee in East Africa when we ran into an American friend of his. Lee's friend began to tease him about his Arabic, a sensitive issue with Lee, as he was very proud of his Arabic skills. Lee tried to stifle the conversation, but his friend would have none of that. I sensed a good laugh and prodded the friend to proceed with his story.

Several months earlier, Lee's friend had come across him at the Khartoum airport, looking dirty and disheveled. Obviously harried, Lee told his friend that he and a co-worker had been lost outside the city. That was not hard to imagine. Khartoum was surrounded by desert, with one direction looking exactly like another and every dirt road seemed to lead to an endless horizon. Driving around lost for hours, Lee and his friend had also lost their bearings back to the airport. With the next flight out days away, they had begun to panic about missing their plane. Spotting an aged Bedouin with his mule by the side of the road, they braked their auto to a screeching stop while creating an enormous cloud of dust. Lee jumped out of the car and, in his most fluent Arabic, asked, "Where's the airport?"

The old man, enveloped in the dust, portrayed a look of puzzlement giving way to bewilderment. The Bedouin raised his arms upward, alternating staring at the sky and Lee, saying nothing.

As Lee related his inquiry of the Bedouin, his friend, truly fluent in Arabic, started to laugh.

His friend roared. "No, no," he said. "You pronounced airport *MAtar*, not *maTAR*. Laughing almost uncontrollably, he explained, "You asked the man 'Where's the rain?' That's why he looked at the sky. Hell, there's been no rain in Sudan for two years." It was indeed a question the old man had probably never been asked in quite that way.

That Bedouin, to this day, is probably mystifying his friends and family with the story about the strange, frantic white man demanding answers to imponderable questions about the vagaries of nature.

Lee, Omar, and I each had our share of the challenges of cross-language communications, but we faced problems from different angles. Our stories illustrate that ensuring adequate translations, understanding culturally rooted language taboos, and avoiding language misunderstandings pay dividends to success.

Cultural Snapshot

I would be remiss if I did not add a French cultural experience that I found to typify many of my experiences in foreign lands. DeGaulle's view of French superiority is very much alive and well and was oh so evident to me in an encounter in a five-star restaurant just off the Champs-Elysées.

It was spring, and the weather was spectacular. My friend Steve and I were seated side by side, rather than facing one another, along the wall of the restaurant. Next to us on either side, other patrons were similarly seated. We ordered, and, after a typical lengthy wait, we were served our food.

Just as our food arrived, the gentleman seated at the adjacent table lit a huge stogie, sending a massive smoke screen billowing across our food. If a bonfire had just been lit at the next table, it couldn't have generated more smoke. The cloud left us coughing and madly trying to fan the smoke away.

Between coughs, I asked Steve—British through and through, yet quite proficient in French—to point out to the man our smoky plight. Steve leaned over to the man very politely and spoke in French for about fifteen seconds. The man looked at Steve expressionless, shrugged, said something very briefly, and let out another billow of smoke.

Steve turned to me and said, "He said, it is not his problem that the wind takes the smoke into our faces." I was stunned. We hurriedly ate our meal, taking bites between the plumes of smoke that continued unabated.

The Harvard Saudi:
A Lesson in Maintaining Face

In another of my trips to Saudi Arabia, I had occasion to deal with a fellow I'll call Dr. Murki. I've changed his name as there is evidence to suggest he has become a high-ranking Saudi diplomat. Now, Murki was very Westernized, suave, and as business savvy as his Harvard education indicated. For over a year, I'd had nothing but the best experiences with Dr. Murki. Because of his education and the way in which he had conducted his affairs, I had thought of him as a Westerner. This view was in spite of the fact that it had been apparent to me for some time that, for many Saudis, the view of non-Saudis was to tolerate them—if they were at least Muslim. If they were non-Saudi *and* non-Muslim, well, they comprised a being only slightly above Little Muffy. Many Saudis were, and remain, by all accounts from my experience, insufferable in their arrogance and condescension.

It came to pass that Dr. Murki became in debt to my company for over sixty thousand dollars due to an extension of credit I had allowed—no good deed ever goes unpunished—and I was duped so thoroughly that I probably should have been fired. In order to collect the debt, I called Murki repeatedly. He did not return any of my calls. Finally, on a trip to Jeddah, I went to his office and confronted him in person. Caught off guard by my presence in Jeddah, Murki told me he had sold his company and assured me that the debt owed to my company would, by contractual arrangement with the new owners, be paid. My fears of nonpayment somewhat assuaged, the meeting actually ended on a friendly note.

The next day, I approached the new owners. During the course of that meeting, I was given information directly counter to what Murki had offered the day before. No contractual arrangement existed, and the new owners clarified that any past debts were still Murki's. It was dawning on me that Murki's story had been completely fabricated. It certainly appeared that, as much as I didn't want to believe it, he had lied to my face.

All my further attempts to meet with or call Murki were fruitless. I was left completely disappointed by the outcome of my collection attempts and by Murki's behavior.

On the flight back to Europe, I related the story in general terms to a craggy businessman. I had often found similar conversations with such old salts very informative, and that was the case this time. The old salt had been doing business in the Middle East for years and relayed to me an insight he had learned. He explained that if you backed a businessman there into a corner, and he lied to you as a result, it was your fault.

Completely confused, I asked what he meant. It all had to do with the Middle Eastern concept of "face," he told me. Clarifying the concept, the old salt suggested that I look at it in Western terms as avoiding any degree of shame or embarrassment. In the Middle East, as well as other places, maintaining face is *everything*—to the extent that lying or cheating, especially when a non-Muslim is involved, are instantly considered moral—if it helps one to avoid losing face. In essence, the concept was intrinsic to the culture.

Talk about a tough way to begin my awareness of the concept of face and its inherent cultural connection! Dr. Murki's lie was my fault by this truism. I had confronted him, certainly shaming him about the debt, and left him no out *but to lie* to me. Never mind that Murki's business ethics were in short supply, the elemental facet of maintaining face was at work here: avoid any level of shame or embarrassment by any means necessary. Had I gone about this differently, the old salt explained, my chances of getting *some* measure of repayment would have been much, much better.

I never recovered the sixty thousand dollars, and it made for a costly beginning to the insights on face as a cultural axiom. The concept of "maintaining face" exists everywhere, although it may manifest itself differently in varying cultures and is usually in play to one degree or another whenever the potential of embarrassment exists.

As with all of my lessons, I found there was still much learn.

The Road to Oz:
A Simple Lesson in Problem Solving

On another visit in 1983, I returned to Saudi Arabia to address problems we were having with the hospital at Al Baja, where that $20 million of medical supplies had been delivered. The problems at the hospital had been evolving for over a year. There had been repeated, unsuccessful attempts via telephone and fax to prevent and solve the ongoing problems. Still, the problems and their potential solutions remained a bit of a mystery. Lee was to join me in a drive up to the hospital to attempt to assuage the hard feelings that had developed.

Lee, antibureaucratic to his very soul, had been in the Kingdom for a year and half, and he still didn't have a Saudi driving permit. The Saudis have a rigid rule that, within one month of entering the Kingdom, you have to obtain a permit, or you cannot drive. Not having one didn't faze Lee in the least, although he was constantly running into trouble because of it—and then talking himself out of it.

We made our way up the sharply ascending escarpment toward the hospital blasting a Bill Withers tape the whole way. The most severe and dangerous part of the escarpment was the ascent to the city of Taif, located on a plateau some four thousand feet up from the Red Sea. Part of the danger was due to the cutback nature of the road carved into the rocky face of the plateau. The road rose steeply via a series of hairpin curves, many of them totally blind to oncoming traffic. The other part of the danger was that the Saudis practiced a form of kamikaze driving coming up and down the escarpment. They just passed at any time. When they guessed wrong, say on a blind curve, horrible accidents occurred. That the gory, head-on collision wreckage was never moved brought the peril into sharp focus. Tons of wreckage—suggesting hundreds of crashes—littered both sides of the road.

Passing through Taif, Lee pulled up to a security checkpoint on the city outskirts. I knew he didn't have a driving permit and wondered how he would wiggle out of this situation. I could imagine us both being detained. Sure enough, after examining Lee's work permit, a guard ordered us out of the car. As always, it was very hot standing in the desert sun. In an incredibly surreal scene, I could hear Bill Withers wailing away "Ain't No Sunshine" on the tape deck as I watched the situation unfold.

As the senior guard verbally berated Lee while simultaneously filling out a report, his pen went dry. Lee casually handed his own pen to the guard. The guard took it and resumed his writing and lecturing. Traffic was backing up significantly, and the guard couldn't help but take notice. These weren't *hawajas*, or Westerners, sitting in their cars idling in the hot sun. There was certainly an important Saudi in one of them who could raise a stink for the delay. The guard suddenly gestured toward Lee's car and told us to just go. Luck had been with us.

When we finally reached the hospital, located so high in the mountains that it sat above the clouds looking a bit like Oz, we had a very surprising meeting with the management group. It was almost immediately evident that many—I would even say most—of the problems the hospital had posed were misdirected. A significant degree of the disaffection that had been growing did not involve our duties whatsoever; rather, it was tied to product-ordering issues with their own headquarters in the United States. It seemed almost unbelievable, but like ships passing in the night, the problems had escalated over practically nothing.

The relief on both sides at the end of the meeting was palpable. The balloon of disenchantment had been popped, and I could not truly claim any degree of merit other than merely showing up. No less a wise soothsayer than Woody Allen has observed, "Eighty percent of success is showing up." I always thought it was a joke, but it seemed he might have had a point.

With the surprising meeting over, Lee drove us back down toward Taif, some two thousand feet below on the narrow, snaking road that had seemed so intimidating on the way up. Now it was worse. I knew that Saudis did not use their headlights at night because they thought headlamps drained truck batteries. Before leaving that morning, I had made a mental note that we should be off the escarpment before the end of daylight. It looked like we had left just enough time to make the journey before the sun set.

I was startled when Lee unexpectedly braked and said, "Man, you have to see these baboons. There's a bunch of them right down there."

He parked along the side of the road and then led me, reluctant, but curious, down a ravine. Not smart, for any number of excellent reasons—we all know what curiosity did for the cat. The ground didn't drop away precipitously, but it was tiered in steppes. We had gone perhaps two hundred yards from the car, far enough that we had lost sight of it, when we suddenly came upon a troop of baboons.

These baboons were roughly four feet tall with yellow teethlike fangs that looked to me, from the stupidly close proximity that I found myself in, to be at least three feet long. We'd apparently not arrived at a good time because their screeches were bloodcurdling. Realizing the sudden peril, we immediately started back toward the car. As we turned, a contingent of baboons started loping after us. We began angling away from those following us, trying to make it up the steppes where we had left Lee's car. Looking down the hill, we could see other baboons moving parallel to us on the lower ground. They seemed to be all around us. A sudden screech sounded like it came from *between* the car and where we stood.

My heart was going absolutely nuts down in that ravine. Our feet barely touched the ground as we bolted toward the road. We jumped into the car and locked the doors like a couple of scared kids. Although we were laughing, it was laughter born from sheer terror, not mirth. We both felt that we narrowly escaped becoming an afternoon snack. The stupidity of our little sojourn along the steppes clearly didn't need to be brought up.

As we continued our way down the remaining escarpment, I realized the risk that imminent darkness would bring and how doubly stupid our little baboon excursion had been. Concerned with the lack of daylight remaining, I wanted to avoid any head-on collisions with the dozens of darkened Saudi trucks that might careen around the blind roadway corners with only Allah as their co-pilot to light the route. We still had to pass through Taif before descending the last and, by far, most hazardous part of the escarpment. I also realized that we had to go back through the same checkpoint! Any delay would certainly result in our descending the escarpment in the dark.

Reaching the checkpoint, it was a case of *déjà vu* all over again. Astonishingly, the very same guard didn't remember us from six hours before. That, in and of itself, was a mystery. The guard told us to get out of the car, ordered Lee to shut off the Withers tape, and, definitely not a good sign, to go with him to the detention area. Lee whispered to me, "I think we're screwed this time." *No shit, Sherlock!* I thought.

The guard marched us toward the barracks when suddenly he stopped and turned. A look of recognition crossed his face—he had serendipitously remembered Lee. Well, not Lee exactly, as hard as that was to fathom. What the guard remembered was that Lee had given him a pen, and, in his haste to see us on our way earlier that day, he had absently kept Lee's pen. An honest Saudi—and despite my experiences to the contrary, there were many of them—this guard suddenly ran to his office and came out waving Lee's pen.

Lee, fortuitously, knew the Arabic word for "gift." He said no, he had not forgotten the pen previously, but it had been meant as a gift for the guard.

Instantaneously, the man's demeanor changed. You'd have thought that the guard had won the lottery.

Immediately, we were honored guests. The guard stopped the other policemen, to their utmost annoyance, who were busy impounding Lee's car. Holding the car door open for us, the guard saluted as we drove off toward Jeddah.

"Holy about face," as Robin might say to Batman. If I hadn't seen it, I wouldn't have believed it. This time it wasn't sheer luck that had allowed us to escape. Accommodation had come into play again—not just the act itself, but the skill with which Lee handled it. This incident served to pique my awareness that an important facet of accommodation is that the offer, the contract execution if you will, cannot carry the connotation of a bribe.

This time the accommodation was not bags of cash or legal tender of any kind. No, an offer of cash probably would have gotten us in real trouble. Accommodation can take many different forms.

Ensh Allah:
A Lesson in Local Logic

The following day, having finally, and safely, arrived back in Jeddah, I discussed the Saudi approach to driving with Lee at length. The night before, my mind had unsuccessfully wrestled with the capriciousness and, to a Western mind, illogical approach Saudis took to driving, especially at night. As it was in so much of Saudi life, I believed it had a great deal to do with the way they chose to apply the teachings of the Muslim religion. The two most common Arabic expressions were *Maleesh*, meaning "don't worry" or "not to worry," and *Ensh Allah* or "God willing."

That second phrase seems to have a profound influence on Arabic life, but its concept is most difficult for a Westerner to grasp. Simply put, everything is in God's hands. It is one of the six articles of faith in Islam. This core tenet strikes me as seeing everything in life as a form of overtly controlled and micromanaged fate. So taking a blind curve isn't lunacy, for all is in the hands of Allah. When a devout Muslim wishes to make a plan, utter a promise, or make a resolution or a pledge, he makes it with the permission and the will of Allah. Muslims are to strive hard, in theory, and put their trust in Allah with whom they leave the ultimate results.

There are two applications of *Ensh Allah*. The first is by the genuinely religious and is faithfully applied as described above. With them, I have no beef. The second is the way the phrase is applied in secular life. Whenever I heard the words *Ensh Allah* spoken just after making important arrangements, say for a truck delivery, I came to understand that was very close to our understanding of "go fly a kite."

You cannot fathom how screwed you can be when you hire a truck driver to haul an important shipment of supplies that must, without fail, be delivered as specified, and the driver looks you square in the eye and utters, *"Ensh Allah."* If you take this as being a substitute for a common courtesy like, "As you wish," then you are well on your way, as I was a few times, to a frustrating insight into a different type of logic. Like the concept of face, logic and how it manifests is intrinsic to culture.

I had never been exposed to such thinking before. In school, we are taught a deductive type of reasoning that leaves most Westerners, Americans particularly, ill equipped to deal with the seemingly non-deductive logic so commonplace in the international environment. I can't begin to count how many Westerners I have seen who have had their spirits and mental outlooks completely shaken by "foreign" logic.

My awareness that logic, as I understood it, could be different, very different, had begun. In "Ensh Allah" situations, an at least a discernable, if not acceptable, logic was at play. I learned later on in my travels that, in various cultures, this wasn't always the case.

The Jeddah Jaywalker:
A Lesson in Jurisprudence

In Saudi Arabia, as in many Muslim countries, Sharia law is the basis of the legal system. Sharia law is based upon the teachings of the Quran, and, under it, the rights of non-Muslims are arguably less than those of Muslims. This general truism carried through the legal system right down to the rights one was accorded while driving in the Kingdom.

When it came to driving in Saudi Arabia, the good news was they drove on the right hand side of the road. That ends the summary of the good news. Most of the streets were fairly wide, if not well marked. Driving about in the cities, you'd find a stoplight with ten cars, if there was room, lined up side by side. If the guy on the far right wanted to make a left, he would turn left in front of everyone else. This maneuver was termed, with sarcastically laced affection, by Westerners as "the Saudi slide." You never knew when a car might come careening out of nowhere and cut right in front of you. You drove or rode in a car in constant fear of the "Saudi slide" or a similarly crazy driving move, accented by the certain knowledge that, if there were an accident, you would be held 100 percent at fault.

Saudi laws, and the way they apply to Westerners, had dire consequences for Rod, our manager in Jeddah. He had the misfortune to accidentally drive into a Hajji—a person on pilgrimage to Mecca—who, we later learned, had never been in a major city before. The Hajji had no experience with city traffic and had unknowingly stepped into the street at an intersection against a red light when Rod struck him.

The resulting legal situation was based upon an interpretation of Sharia law. Because Rod was a foreigner in the Kingdom, a *non-Muslim* foreigner at that, the accident was Rod's fault. If he hadn't been there, occupying that space in time in a Muslim country, the accident would never have taken place. All this had to be taken with a heavy dose of the Saudi disdain for foreigners. Sharia law dictated that not only must reparations be paid to the Hajji's family and his hospital bills taken care of, but Rod also had to spend the exact amount of time in a Jeddah jail that it took for the Hajji to be released from the hospital—three and a half weeks. The day the Hajji left the hospital, Rod left the jail.

The Jeddah jail was brutal, right out of the film *Midnight Express*. There was no food fit to eat, and Rod spent the endless days in a crowded, filthy cell. After learning about the dearth of edible food, Lee brought Rod meals and water for the duration of his imprisonment. Even with the delivery of proper sustenance, Rod emerged from the jail twenty pounds lighter.

Rod was very lucky the Hajji was not mortally injured. He could have faced a consequence as severe as death.

Cultural Snapshot

As one might expect, the many maddening frustrations Westerners encounter in Saudi Arabia result in various kinds of backlash. The most extreme one I heard about took place in the Western compounds in the eastern province, in the town of Al Kobar.

Most of the "infidels" were, of course, Americans or Europeans who had never been treated as second-class citizens in their own countries. If one wants to get a sense of what Blacks, Hispanics, or any other historically discriminated group might feel in America, they need only to spend a brief time in Saudi Arabia. One of the reactions to the harsh Saudi social attitudes and the frustrating environment was the so-called Bash-a-Saudi clubs.

The clubs functioned like this: to be a full member you had to encounter a Saudi and tackle him or deck him with a punch to the jaw or chest. Of course, to avoid a lengthy jail sentence or even death, you had to deck your target outside of the Kingdom.

Once the Saudi was sprawled on the ground, the attacker had to take a photograph, in those days a Polaroid, as proof. Showing that photo in any Western compound in Saudi Arabia would get you free drinks or even dinner.

European Faux Pas:
A Lesson in Blending In

In addition to the strange predicaments Lee and I seemed to be constantly stumbling into, changing world events inserted an element of instability and peril into our travels.

In 1985, while in New York on my way to Scandinavia, a friend's wife asked me if I was concerned, since I traveled so often to places where Americans were being targeted by terrorists. The honest answer was that I hadn't given the matter much thought, but her question caused me to realize that I probably needed to do just that.

Anti-Americanism was thriving in the Muslim world, and terrorism was becoming a constant threat to Americans overseas. In 1983, a truck bomb had devastated the Marine barracks in Lebanon, resulting in a total withdrawal of the American forces there. Two years later, terrorists seized the cruise liner *Achille Lauro* and pushed a wheelchair-bound American passenger overboard, killing him. That same year a TWA passenger jet was hijacked and an American serviceman brutally murdered, his body thrown onto an airport tarmac by the terrorists. Then American journalist Terry Anderson was kidnapped and held hostage in Beirut, and the entire country of Lebanon became engulfed in civil war.

All these incidents served to highlight the increasing anti-American sentiment, not just in the Middle East, but even throughout Europe where terrorist cells were operating as well. Anti-Americanism and the terrorists sowing this sentiment were in the newspaper headlines and on the network news broadcasts constantly. I was suddenly aware of the red bulls-eye that Americans traveling abroad, and especially in the Middle East, had figuratively painted on them, and I began to take a series of precautions to avoid being targeted.

My first safety measure was to begin trying to appear as someone not American. I took to wearing turtleneck sweaters and white socks. It was a strange fashion statement of the day, but Europeans had taken to wearing white socks with every type of casual and formal wear, even suits. I caught plenty of flak in the United States before departure for this fashion faux pas, but on the road, I reasoned, no self-respecting terrorist could think I was anything but European. I flew KLM or Lufthansa whenever possible, instead of an American airline. Such a masquerade in transit was about all I could do, but at least it was something. Every savvy American traveling overseas was worried. Many took the same steps of being discreet, not attracting attention, and avoiding any appearance blatantly American in order to be as inconspicuous as possible.

In addition to the anti-Americanism I had experienced, there had also been some very real travel-related health issues that had raised their grisly presence. The first occasion had been in Saudi Arabia. I had been very thirsty on arrival and opened a bottle of orange juice from a hotel room refrigerator. It didn't taste right going down—it kind of made my throat tickle. I felt no immediately reaction, but that night, I got the sweats, followed by a low-grade fever. For that entire trip, I could not turn my days and nights around. I had a beer once or twice, and it just about knocked me out.

Back in the States, I felt bad for weeks and even the smell of beer made me feel ill. Astonishing even myself, I stopped drinking it altogether for a while. With only the "bulletproof" mentality that twenty-somethings exude, I never thought about going to the doctor. After a month to six weeks, I finally started to feel better. The fever and sweats went away, and I put it out of my mind.

Not long afterward, I had a series of routine blood tests during an insurance-mandated physical and was asked if I'd ever had jaundice. I told the doctor I had not. Then he asked if I'd ever had a low-grade fever that wouldn't go away. I told him about what had happened in Saudi Arabia. "That was a mild case of hepatitis," the doctor said, "and you were very lucky."

Needless to say, from that point on, I was very careful about what I ate or drank. A major component of staying healthy was to eat only well-cooked food, eat breads as much as possible, stay away from eating fruits and produce, and to be very careful of everything I drank.

The regions of the world where I spent a great amount of time were known for striking Westerners with various debilitating diseases, and hepatitis was common. To be safe, I kept abreast of all necessary inoculations, even those for influenza, and preventative medications, such as antimalarial drugs.

Because I conscientiously held to these rules regarding foods, inoculations, and preventative medications, illness was a travel complication that did not plague me often. I was only really sick three times in over one hundred international trips.

The Masai Lion Guide:
A Lesson in Using Your
Mind and Trusting Your Gut

In early 1986, I scheduled a trip to Africa that was my first extended tour of that marvelous continent.

My first stop on this trip was Abidjan, the Paris of West Africa. Lee met me in London and joined me for the trip to investigate various business opportunities. We spent two sweaty days in a very humid Abidjan and then flew on to Nairobi, via Kinshasa, on Ethiopian Airways. The meetings in Abidjan were uninformative, and we hoped the meetings in Nairobi and finally Khartoum would be more fruitful.

The trip to Nairobi was off to an inauspicious start when one of the passengers attempting to cook a meal on a Bunsen burner–type apparatus caused a small fire in the plane's cabin.

After my first few steps off the plane in Nairobi, I had realized I was short of breath and learned that the city was at over six thousand feet in elevation. The land was lush with palm trees and was quite beautiful. After the energy-sapping heat and humidity of Abidjan, Nairobi was a pleasant and welcome change. We had arrived during the wet season, and clouds rolled in over the vast plains, dumping rain every day. They left behind brilliant sunlight and a crisp, refreshing, nearly chilly air, scrubbed clean of all the dust and emissions of city traffic. The smell was intoxicating, and it seemed I could see for a thousand miles.

The hotel sector downtown was fairly modern. There were the usual American chains: Sheraton, Hilton, Hyatt, etc., all there to support tourists flocking to go on safari. Lee and I, en route from the airport to the Hilton, realized we were just south of the equator. Like college freshmen away from home for the first time, the first thing we did after arriving in our rooms was to flush the toilet to see if the water really did swirl the opposite direction. When it did, we high-fived while flushing again and again.

The meetings in Nairobi were not any more informative than the Abijan meetings had been. After breakfast on the morning of our departure to Khartoum, I was in my room packing when I happened to see a flash bulletin on television preempting the regular Reuters news feed. The headlines streaming across the bottom of the screen were garish: "U.S. Declares War on Libya." Incorrect, of course, but I didn't know that then. This was back before CNN.

I called Lee's room and asked, "Have you heard? The U.S. is at war with Libya!"

Lee was stunned at the news, though tension with Libya had been growing. I asked him if he thought we should go to Khartoum. He had been there many times and said that he didn't think that two Americans would have trouble.

My gut was trying to tell me something. I felt I knew more than my memory was reminding me and that sense was compelling me not to go to Khartoum. After some reflection, I told Lee there was no way of knowing what the next few days would bring. I hated to sound overcautious, but that was exactly how it seemed. We extended our reservations at the hotel and booked a flight to Cairo the following day.

We had a day to kill in Kenya. The 120-square-kilometer Nairobi Game Park was situated just outside the city so, mimicking the tourists, we decided to go on safari. Before leaving the hotel we hired a guide, a tall, lanky Masai, to take us on a tour of the game park that afternoon. There we saw a dizzying panorama of gazelles, antelopes, zebras, giraffes, water buffalos, and more. Between the animals and the spectacular scenery, it was breathtaking. Finally, very late that afternoon the guide, whose English was decent, asked, "Hippo?"

"Why not?" we asked. "Let's go." After a short drive off the main roadway, the guide stopped the vehicle and said to us, "Hippo in creek. Long way. Must walk."

It took about thirty-five minutes trekking through the bush to reach the creek while the setting sun was casting ever-lengthening shadows. Abruptly, our guide looked around in comprehension and came to a halt. In an urgent voice he said, "Very sorry. No hippo." Without further warning or explanation, he turned and bolted back the way we had just come. Lee and I looked at each other bewildered. We shouted after the fast moving Masai, "Hey! What's the rush?"

The guide yelled back over his shoulder, arms and legs pumping for all they were worth, "Must run now. Sun go down. Lions come!"

Unfortunately, that made sense. Jungle lore had it that lions came out at twilight to drink from the creek and to hunt the animals doing the same. Suddenly, we were like two cartoon characters. We did a double take, our eyes growing round in comprehension. *Lions come? Holy shit!*

We took off in panic. We were nearly two miles from the van. As we ran, it occurred to us that it was very likely that the lions might well use the very route we were on to reach the creek. Apparitions of lions seemed to appear everywhere in the elongated shadows of the setting sun.

In my terror, I recalled our previous experience with the rampaging baboons and wondered if fortune would favor us twice. It took us twenty terrorized minutes to reach our vehicle. When we arrived sweating, panting from exhaustion, the guide who'd arrived well ahead of us was securely situated inside the vehicle.

Heaving for breath, we were angry at the stupidity, the lack of forethought causing the situation. I began to scold the guide. Amazingly, the guide was genuinely surprised at our anger.

It was my first potentially dire experience with the apparent complete absence of logic. The eventuality that we would reach the stream at sundown was not probable, hell it was absolute. Very simply, the deduction I would have assumed was automatic, from the guide's cultural standpoint, was not. This Masai guide had given no thought at all to a probable and potentially grave danger. As the sun went down, the guide's realization was like a caveman discovering fire for the first time. Culturally, our logic was as different as night and day.

Back at the hotel the scene was complete chaos. Frantic Westerners and their luggage jammed the lobby when we entered. Making our way to the elevator, I asked an attractive young woman if this was a Safari contingent. She smiled wearily and shook her head "no." They were evacuees from Khartoum. She explained that earlier that morning, after the American attack on Tripoli, two embassy employees had been shot. One of them, the embassy's communications officer, was in serious condition. Westerners were considered targets and all nonessential embassy personnel had been hurriedly evacuated to Nairobi.

I was suddenly aware that, by virtue of my gut feeling, we had avoided flying into a firestorm. I could not have known that there had been attacks on the U.S. Embassy in Khartoum, and I do not make claim to some type of extra sensory perception (ESP), but it was clear that I occasionally got a sense of direction that was not concretely explainable. Over time, I begrudgingly accepted this sense as intuition. As the full implications of what she was relating hit home, Lee and I looked at one another wide-eyed.

We skipped the elevator and made our way straight to the bar.

Sign of the Times

After finally departing Nairobi for Cairo, the only time Lee got me out of the hotel was to visit the Pyramids. The entire area around Cheops, the largest of the Pyramids, and the nearby Sphinx was deserted. Due to the hostilities in Libya, not a Western soul was about. I asked Lee if he was worried about the potential for harm. Lee, who was shorter than me, swarthy, and could probably easily pass muster as an Arab, replied that as long as I was with him he felt quite safe. Knowing this could not possibly be a gratuitous compliment, I bit and asked, "Why is that?" He smiled and said he could point to me and say, "Shoof," *American*. "Allah Akbar!" *God is Great!* Terrorists would be so thrilled to have such an obvious hawaja in their midst that they surely wouldn't bother with Lee. What a buddy!

Out of India:
Lessons in Accommodation and Negotiation

By 1986, it was painfully obvious that the company I worked for, Four Winds, was close to going bankrupt. I wanted to be back on the East Coast when that occurred, so I arranged to be transferred to the company office in Alexandria, Virginia, just outside of Washington DC.

As the company continued to financially spiral downward, plans—largely formed over drinks in a bar—were made to begin a start up company. Within six months of my arrival on the East Coast, I, along with three partners, launched a new company we named Matrix. Turning bar talk into reality proved to be filled with invaluable insights that would eventually pay major dividends.

There were many countries that became vital to the growth of the new company, but none more essential than India. I knew nothing of this heavily populated country of the Asian subcontinent, so I headed there first.

For the first time in a long while, India was making the right sounds to the U.S. government, and there was the feeling that the country was finally turning a cold shoulder to the Soviets. In return for this positive sign, U.S. humanitarian assistance to India had been resumed. The initial programs were primarily agriculture related, with the focus on modern irrigation techniques.

Doing business in India was particularly complex. The historic Indian bureaucracy was a maze that had been complicated, if not wholly instituted, by the long British presence. As a result, its customs authority is possibly the most Byzantine in the world, even worse than Egypt.

My first trip to New Delhi resulted in information so useless that I made plans to immediately return, determined to stay there until I got facts that made sense. In my efforts to uncover relevant information, I fortuitously arranged a meeting with an agent in Bombay, now known as Mumbai.

I had arrived during the rainy season. Typical of many places in Asia, the bulk of annual rainfall—in Bombay a torrential one hundred inches—falls during the monsoons, making the days dreary and steamy. Well, fate or the angels were kind to me in Bombay, a teeming megalopolis that is the financial center of India. There I met a fellow named Willie, the owner of an Indian transportation company. Willie, tall with dark curly hair, impeccably courteous, and carrying a faint resemblance to Omar Sharif, became a lifelong friend and valuable business partner.

I will never forget the morning when Willie and his brother explained to me the surreal and complicated nature of Indian customs. This was comparable in effect to a layman's explanation of quantum mechanics. Suddenly, I "got" it. Thanks to them, I understood the entire morass of the Alice in Wonderland nature of India's import paperwork.

This meeting with Willie and his brother was also a revelation to the understanding of how all developing countries work. It even helped to put together tidbits of information I had learned in Egypt and Saudi Arabia in prior years. I saw a process—an intentionally complicated one—that I could navigate. To explain everything Willie told me that morning would be lengthy and boring, but there were two main points that were valuable to me in conducting my business around the world.

First, all developing countries possess currencies that are soft. This implies that the government, as opposed to the currency having a market-based value, sets the monetary values artificially. Unilaterally, countries having soft currencies base their duties, fines, penalties, etc. on imports in hard currencies like dollars or euros. Essentially, the importation process in any developing country is a game designed to squeeze out the greatest amount of hard currency possible.

Second, the procedural and paperwork games that arise out of this hard currency obsession created an aspect that made me uncomfortable: I realized that accommodation was a big part of this game. The scene I had witnessed in Taif with Mohammed and his cousin was far more the norm than the exception. While I had always known there were accommodations being made, I didn't think it was to this scale. Not that the money exchanging hands was extreme, often it was only a few dollars, but it was the fact that it *always* occurred that was such an epiphany.

This eye-opening experience occupied my thoughts as I returned to the United States from that trip. I knew peripherally of a law called the Foreign Corrupt Practices Act (FCPA), but I didn't really know what it encompassed. There on the plane, I made a mental promise to familiarize myself with the law as soon as I got back to the States.

My initial investigation educated me on the intent of the law. In the 1970s, the U.S. Government learned that hundreds of U.S. companies routinely made off-the-books payments, i.e., bribes, to foreign companies and officials. The FCPA was enacted to bring a halt to that practice by U.S.

companies. The law goes so far as to specify that it is illegal to even know about such a payment, made on behalf of a U.S. company by a third party. Given my indirect involvement in the Indian payments, that part concerned me.

Conducting business outside the United States required specific and comprehensive understanding of what constituted illegal bribery and what constituted permissible accommodation. I sought to familiarize myself with the specifics of the FCPA and found a section of the law that defined permissible payments. This section specifically stated that "facilitating" payments, accommodations in my jargon, were an explicit exception for "routine governmental action" such as obtaining permits, loading and unloading cargo, and scheduling inspections associated with transit of goods. Whew, I was absolutely in the clear.

Before leaving on any trip I prepared a list of locations where we were working or hoping to work. Then, sitting down with the Overseas Airline Guide, I plotted a route that would take me to every important destination within a reasonable time frame. I had learned from experience this was twenty to thirty days. Much longer and I turned into a walking zombie. Sleep deprivation and jet lag were constant problems, and I have yet to find satisfactory solutions.

On a visit to Hyderabad, India, the effects of these problems caught up with me. The purpose of the trip was to attend a meeting at the headquarters of an agricultural institute and negotiate a contract with its director. I met Willie in the Bombay airport within hours of my arrival from London. I was only able to catch about three hours sleep, my first vertical shut-eye in almost thirty-six hours, before the early morning flight to Hyderabad.

When we arrived at the institute, I was simply dead tired and groggy. I had hoped to meet with the director immediately and then undertake whatever traditional pleasantries they had planned. Well, that was not to be. Willie and I were kept waiting in a guesthouse on the outskirts of the institute for the entire morning. Around noon, we were ushered to meet the director and then taken immediately to a sumptuous lunch. After a delicious meal of local Indian cuisine, we were escorted on a two-hour tour of the institute.

I was barely able to keep my eyes open. The wait in the guesthouse had seemed interminable. After the huge lunch, I was a walking zombie. Finally, at five o'clock that evening—a good nine hours after our arrival—Willie and I were led to the director's office to meet and negotiate.

To say my memory of those negotiations is fuzzy would be an understatement. In that meeting with the institute director, I was barely aware of my name much less any leverage I might gain. After brief negotiations and summary agreement, Willie and I left immediately to catch the last flight of the day back to Bombay.

During the plane boarding, Willie gently inquired if I knew to what I'd agreed. I said I did. He then expressed concern. "I didn't want to say anything during negotiations," he said. "It wasn't my place." Over the next few minutes, he carefully outlined the awful predicament I had created.

A key element in the negotiations had been amounts of cargo weighed in kilos. I was so weary that I had not properly calculated in my head the conversions from kilos into pounds. Worse, when we'd discussed converting monetary sums from English pounds into American dollars, I had really messed up good. As Willie assessed the correct conversions, I grasped the dilemma. In my miserable condition, I'd verbally committed to an impossible pricing arrangement. Feeling inept, naïve, foolish, and humiliated, I knew I had only one course of action.

The next day I called the director from Bombay and shamefully admitted my error. I explained I could not possibly abide by the terms to which I had so willingly agreed. You can't imagine how stupid it felt to actually say it.

Surprisingly, the objections were only half-hearted. Though not admitting it, the director and his staff surely had known the agreement was impossible. The Indians had known my travel itinerary—heck I had sent it to them—and had purposely dragged Willie and me around all day, delaying the negotiations for when we'd be exhausted. I firmly believe they only regretted stacking the negotiation scenario too heavily in their favor. They had actually set me up too well.

I realized I had just received an important insight into negotiation from some real pros. Normally, I'd have had no difficulty making either of the mental calculations required during the negotiations. Ignoring my past ignominious experiences with jet lag and coherent thinking, I had allowed jet lag to become a factor in that negotiation. I made the vow to never, ever negotiate when I was jet lagged, tired, or less than my best. This experience made me aware that if I was not awake enough, or well enough, to concentrate on the intricacies of leverage, then I was well on my way to similarly embarrassing thumpings. It was a valuable lesson in negotiation.

Mujahideen and Martial Law: A Lesson in Civil Strife

Being an expert in shipping to the worst regions of the world became my *raison d'etre*. The initial stages of my first entrepreneurial pursuit took me to some of the most strife-torn countries in the world. Many of the countries I visited in the late 1980s were veritable incubators of repression, civil strife, and war. These included places like Pakistan and Sri Lanka, where violence was a part of daily life, as well as Burma and Somalia, where oppression hung in the air like a dense fog. However, as in India, that's where the business was.

At the time, the U.S. government was running supplies of every kind through Pakistan to Afghan rebels, the Mujahideen, in their war against the Soviets. The Soviet Union had invaded Afghanistan in 1979, and the purpose was purportedly a step toward a warm-water port. This made Pakistan the next logical domino of the Communist expansion. The Pakistanis took their plight as a probable eventual target seriously and enthusiastically allowed their country to be used as a transit supply base for the Afghan resistance. As a result, the U.S. government set up a civilian operation in Pakistan very much like they one they'd had two decades before in Vietnam.

Our initial contracts in Pakistan were related to supplying the Mujahideen with the nonlethal supplies being sent into the war zone. The cargoes we handled contained no weapons or ammunition but comprised about everything else you'd need to run a war. There were large shipments of medical supplies, stretchers, bandages, and frozen food to name just a few. It was all part of the U.S. support and funding described in the book and later film starring Tom Hanks, *Charlie Wilson's War*.

I made four trips in quick succession to Pakistan, following up on the steady pipeline of business we had obtained for the Afghan Mujahideen war effort. It was impossible to miss a distinct "edginess" to Pakistan, especially in the major port city of Karachi. A crowded, dusty metropolis, Karachi was home to nearly ten million people, and almost a dozen languages were officially recognized there. Not only was there the Afghan war effort to the north, but also the constant skirmishes with India over territory that had been disputed since the creation of Pakistan in 1947. As a result, Pakistan had all the makings of a country on a very short fuse.

On a return trip to the United States, I was scheduled out from Karachi to Europe on a midmorning flight. I left the Sheraton hotel—the same hotel where four U.S. citizens were gunned down a few years later—early. The route from the Sheraton to the airport passed over a long bridge suspended above an area of Karachi commonly known as Faisalabad. I was told the name developed because of the large donations made by the King of Saudi Arabia to the mainly refugee population camped out there. Here, in years to come, fundamentalist schools called madrasas, financially supported by the Saudis, would sculpt and educate many future terrorists.

This area was a powder keg due to the influx of Iranian refugees from the 1979 overthrow of the Shah and the now steady flow of refugees from the war in Afghanistan. Both groups were infringing on what few jobs were available to the local Pakistanis and threatening already precarious livelihoods. As a result, the encampment had a very low flash point.

That morning there had been an eruption of violence in Faisalabad. The Pakistani army was out in force and had closed down the bridge on the route to the airport. The taxi approached the bridge on the narrow, two-lane road, and the driver slowed to a stop, rolling down his window to speak with the soldier halting traffic. As he did, automatic weapons fire erupted nearby, not exactly a calming sound. It sounded so close that both the driver and I reflexively ducked our heads.

Even with the large Pakistani army presence, bad things can happen very fast in that part of the world. It only took my mind a nanosecond to flip through news accounts of similar events with disastrous endings. Such unrest usually had an alarming way of turning against any Westerner unfortunate enough to be handy.

My first thought was for my immediate safety. My second, to wonder if I'd make the airplane. If there was going to be an upheaval of civil unrest in Karachi, and that's exactly how it looked, then I wanted my keester firmly planted in an airplane seat, departing that city.

The taxi sat for half an hour as traffic steadily backed up, and the air shattered from time to time with more gunfire. Just as I had resigned myself to returning to the Sheraton, the army began to escort passenger cars across the bridge. My taxi was among the first group to be escorted across. Reaching the apex of the overpass with nothing but open road ahead, I told my driver there was an extra fifty dollars in it for him if he made double time to the airport. He did, earning his bonus, and I barely, but gratefully, made my plane.

Sri Lanka's proximity to both Pakistan and India made it relatively easy to work in a visit from either country. The island nation, formerly known as

Ceylon, is a lush, green country famous for its idyllic tea plantations in the mountains and miles and miles of beautiful, sandy beaches. It also possesses, especially in the outskirts of Colombo, the capital, some of the worst potholed, narrow, semipaved roads I've ever seen.

I didn't know it until after I arrived, but the country was constantly boiling in a state of civil unrest. I was shocked to read in the morning paper about almost daily massacres. For more than a decade, the Buddhist Sri Lankan government had been engaged in a war against the Tamil Tigers, a Hindu nationalist group, in the north of the country.

Just before my initial visit, there had been another slaughter. The Indo-Sri Lanka Accord—in which India had promised to help keep peace between the two groups—had just been signed. As a result, there were two Indian battleships anchored just off the line of modern hotels in Colombo. You would think such large warships couldn't anchor that close to the beach, but they had. It was a disconcerting scene to say the least.

The underlying political unrest evident during that first visit would percolate to a dangerous level and erupt a few years later.

When I arrived in Burma later that summer, I knew the country had been under military rule for many years, twenty-six to be exact. The newspapers were regularly updating the political unrest that had begun that March with massive student protests. Additionally, the government had demonetized the economy, which was the spark setting off the demonstrations. When I arrived in the tropical, lush capital of Rangoon, schools were closed, and martial law was in effect.

The absence of children in the streets and the utter lack of laughter anywhere caused me to feel as if I'd entered the Twilight Zone. No one I encountered, not even locals employed at the American Embassy, would discuss the political situation. The sense of fear was pervasive. The genocide that had recently taken place in Cambodia by the Khmer Rouge caused me to wonder if something similar was about to happen in Burma.

It should come then as no surprise that the living conditions were simply dreadful. The only hotel worth using, I was told, was The Strand. Once a splendid example of British colonial architecture, it was now dilapidated, bug infested, and mildew-encrusted. Most of the city fit this description.

My three days in Rangoon passed like three months. Finally, boarding my departing flight, I felt as if I was being released from prison.

Just months later, the situation in Burma erupted into more mass demonstrations by students and democracy advocates. Thousands were killed with the estimates varying from three to ten thousand. The protest leaders that were not killed were jailed by the new military junta. The imprisonment of Aung San Suu Kyi became front page news in papers all over the world for the next few years.

A similarly tense experience came when, during a month-long business trip across Africa and Asia, I traveled to Mogadishu, Somalia. Once again, I missed a country erupting in civil strife by only a short period of time.

Mogo was in a class by itself—hot, dirty, and surprisingly tiny for a city getting so much international attention. As is often the problem when traveling to such hell-holes, flights were infrequent. This was a common difficulty. I had two days of meetings, yet could not get a flight out for five days. Inevitably, I found myself with lots of downtime.

I arrived in Mogo near the end of the twenty-one year rule of Said Barre, a period marked by brutal oppression and government-sponsored murder. Like Burma, the absence of laughter and a sense of palpable fear were evident in the local Somalis. Accordingly, I spent my spare time staying close to the Al Maka Hotel. I was surprised to find that the Italians had settled in this part of Africa. The hotel restaurant served good cappuccino and pasta. Talk about the proverbial oasis in the middle of a desert.

The Al Maka was just off the main traffic circle leading to the airport and only a couple of hundred yards from the Olympic Hotel. This area was to become infamous not long after for the military battle that the movie *Black Hawk Down* was based upon. When Barre was finally driven from power in January 1991, a descent into anarchy followed, leading to the U.S. military involvement and the famous street battles on which the film was based. From the sense of oppression evident during my visit, it seemed preordained that ruinous civil strife was shortly in store for this country.

I came to accept civil tension and upheaval as an unavoidable consequence of the global travel I had to undertake. If any of these areas had become "hot," I should have had a plan. I didn't—and this shortcoming would soon become a specter to deal with.

Cultural Snapshot

These areas of the world also offered some rather bizarre sights, and one in Mogadishu was among the most bizarre. To kill time in Mogo one day, I had walked down to the spectacular beaches that lay just a few hundred yards down from the Al Maka. The beaches were as beautiful as any in the world I had ever seen, yet they were completely deserted.

I found out that during the early 1970s the Somalis had enjoyed a close relationship with the Soviets. With typical Soviet disregard for human concerns, they had opened a meatpacking plant a mile or so up from the city center. It was located on a peninsula that formed a natural and particularly gorgeous bay. The plant dumped an enormous quantity of meat residue, untreated of course, directly into the ocean. As a result, tens of thousands of hungry sharks were attracted right up to the shallowest waters of that beach.

Every local knew a swimmer wouldn't last a minute in anything more than ankle deep water. There were no signs of warning anywhere.

Dakar Nights:
A Lesson in Dealing
with Dangerous Destinations

The African continent was one I always enjoyed—a source of many insights. Two separate arrivals, one in Kinshasa, Zaire and the second in Dakar, Senegal reinforced the importance of being aware of my surroundings when I traveled.

Upon arrival in Kinshasa, Zaire, a friend and I handed over our passports in the airport arrivals hall for the customs immigration process. It was one of the shabbiest airports I'd seen in Africa. The rest of my impressions of Zaire, incredible poverty with disease rampant in the open sewers running throughout the city, were among the worst I'd seen in Africa. Although we were among the first in line, we were the last of some two hundred passengers to clear immigration and have our passports returned. When we stepped outside, expecting to find a taxi, the area surrounding the airport exit was completely deserted. We had landed around four o'clock in the morning, and dawn was just breaking.

We were discussing this unusual situation when a Westerner appeared suddenly from around a corner of the dilapidated building. The Westerner, instantly recognizable by his dress even in the faint light, was moving hurriedly, crouched low to the ground, toward us. Rounding the corner, he was startled to see us. "What are you guys doing here?" he asked in a gruff, forced whisper that was obviously American English.

"Looking for a taxi," I said casually, but also with a degree of bewilderment.

"Didn't anyone tell you that bandits and thieves hang out here? They're in cahoots with the immigration officials inside who make sure the Westerners are the last to exit."

Instinctively edging back toward the wall of the structure, we allowed the alarming message to sink in. The Westerner, now stopped yet still crouching, told us he was a missionary and was waiting to meet his family. "Follow me," our benefactor said. "I'll give you a ride to the hotel."

Still crouched over he headed to his car. Although alarmed, the gravity of the situation had not dawned on me. I asked why he was crouched down.

"Sometimes the bandits shoot first."

Instantly my friend and I bent over, infantry style, and scanned the dimly lit surroundings for human forms. Following our new buddy, we moved quickly away from the terminal exit. Within a minute a van appeared and we all jumped inside.

In the van, the man described how Westerners were routinely robbed or kidnapped from the airport. My friend and I looked at each other wide-eyed, both of us stunned at the developments of the last few minutes. Reaching our hotel and bidding adieu to our new buddy, we realized how fortunate we had been to cross paths with him by such chance. It was to that point the most frightening moment of my travels.

Typical of my hard-headed, two-by-four learning predisposition, this instance did not resolve itself into an issue I should address. I was pretty well-versed and experienced in traveling around the world, or so I thought, and viewed this instance as an anomaly. I would soon find out how wrong I was on all counts.

For all the anxiety I had experienced, I found a pleasant side of world traveling. Simply put, it wasn't all work and no play. Occasionally, I enjoyed some wonderfully memorable moments. A trip to Dakar, Senegal had elements of both. For no particular reason I could discern, Dakar, Senegal had become an important destination. There we had all the problems I'd seen in the other African countries. We were operating four different contracts, and it was time I went.

I arrived in Dakar just after midnight and, as had become de rigueur, finished the entry process at about two o'clock in the morning. Gathering my bags, I went outside. The only taxis available all had two persons in them. I hailed one and, in doing so, was about to get both a postponed realization of and an immediate addition to my travel insights.

After the long flights from the States, and as usual, I was absolutely exhausted. Entering the taxi, I glanced at the smiling driver and his grinning buddy. Departing we cleared the airport area and pulled onto a typical African highway—dark, badly paved, narrow, and potholed.

If you've never been in an area similarly undeveloped, you just can't imagine how black the night can be. This night was slightly overcast, blocking the moon and stars—absolutely without light. Everything beyond and to the sides of the headlights was dark as dark could be.

We soon came to a fork in the road with a crooked, dilapidated signpost that looked like something out of an old horror movie. The sign indicated that Dakar was to the right. We went left. Immediately, an adrenaline surge brought me to full alert. I turned to double check the signpost, but it was enveloped in the darkness as soon as the headlights swung away.

My mind raced. Paranoid to a degree only jet lag can induce, I began to plan my actions. I reasoned in my jet-lagged state of mind that I could take them both. I would first try to break the passenger's neck—such was my panicked reasoning—and then deal with the driver. I tried to get my bearings on exactly the route we had taken from the airport so I could at least return there after taking command of the taxi.

No more than a minute passed, although in my agitated state it seemed like an eternity, as I slowly positioned my bags so I would have unimpeded access to the guy in the passenger seat. The car was moving at a fast clip, and I was worried that the driver might go off the road as I made my move on the passenger.

I waited perhaps another minute. I wanted the car to slow slightly. I thought I noticed the driver and passenger exchange knowing looks. I felt I had to make my move quickly. Just as I was leaning forward in my seat to strike we slowed to round a curve. Straightening back out of the curve, lights appeared ahead. I squinted to see what they were. I realized we were entering Dakar.

I can't describe the wave of relief that passed over me. I sat back in my seat with my heart racing and couldn't help but laugh out loud at myself. Both the passenger and driver turned, looked at me quizzically, and then smiled as if sharing the joke. If they only knew what had been about to happen! As they dropped me off at the Dakar Hilton, my heart was still pounding. I made a mental note to check out the sign that had been the cause of this near catastrophe as I left town.

The following morning, I gathered my notes for the day's meetings and departed the hotel. I found downtown Dakar, the oldest city in French Africa, to be a bit like a southern European city where the skyscrapers were intermixed with the white colonial buildings and villas. The outskirts were quite different, taking on the look and feel of just about anywhere else in Africa—poor, crowded, with ramshackle open-air structures the norm.

When I returned to the hotel, it was not quite dinnertime so I decided to have a drink in the lobby bar. I was just savoring the taste of a nice cold beer when four young women entered the bar. They sat down at the table next to me. Never one to pass on such good fortune, I offered to buy them drinks.

As one beer turned into three, and then four, I was particularly attracted to the shorthaired brunette. Her name was Elaine, and she had an accent that I couldn't quite place. It didn't sound French, so I inquired. It turned out she was Hungarian. Years later, as I began my travels into Hungary and other

Iron Curtain countries, I found that her striking beauty was not uncommon there.

The last evening in Dakar, Elaine and I wound up on an outside terrace bar after seeking asylum from the smoky hotel nightclub where everyone had ventured to take in a pseudo-African, pseudo-French, pseudo-rock-and-roll band. We sat on the terrace overlooking the pool and cliffs that dropped away to the softly lit ocean, shimmering in the bright moonlight.

We spent quite a while there on the terrace, and I sheepishly told her of my ride in from the airport. Elaine was in stitches laughing at the newspaper headlines that would have assuredly appeared somewhere: "Crazed American Attacks Taxi Driver, Sentenced to Death" or the imagined follow up story, "Why Americans Can't Tell Directions." We were together until about five o'clock the next morning when I grudgingly left her.

I left the hotel only three hours after bidding adieu to Elaine, alert enough to remember to watch for the signpost that had so nearly brought me to the brink of an international incident. When I reached the infamous fork in the road, I asked the driver to slow down so I could turn to inspect the sign. Sure enough, and thankfully to my sanity, the signs, obvious in broad daylight, were broken and crossed.

It dawned on me, yes, rather late, that I needed to thoroughly investigate the arrival to each new destination. Also, based on my experience in Dakar and other horror stories I heard, I concluded I should not ride in a taxi occupied by anyone other than the driver. And, from that point on, if I were arriving in the middle of the night, I either had someone known to me, or a hotel representative, meet me. These precautions ensured I had fewer "exciting" arrivals.

Nigerian Shakedown:
A Lesson in Fraud

Two other countries I visited numerous times were replete with challenges and experiences, adding to my growing lexicon of globetrotting lessons. Nigeria and Indonesia could hardly be farther apart in geography, culture, or enjoyment. They are not quite the polar opposites of say Thailand and Nigeria, but they're close.

Consider the Mohammed Murtala Airport near Lagos, Nigeria. Warning signs had been posted around the world for years cautioning travelers that the airport didn't meet minimum security standards. Stepping off the plane on my first visit, I could not believe the open, semiofficial, mugging that took place. The role of customs and of the police, I soon realized, was to rip people off. Making the situation worse, Lagos was absolutely wretched, simply God-awful. With its downtown skyscrapers and decently modern roadways, it appeared to be like most other African port cities. Man, it was not. Chicanery and outright lawlessness dominated every aspect of being.

Departure from the country was even worse. On my way out, I saw nothing "semi" about the official shakedown I received while passing through the customs and immigration exit process. I was simply relieved of all local currency, nira, and any other currency that could be found. I had been warned to hide my dollars, so I made it through without any great loss.

Perhaps a year after that first visit to Nigeria in 1987, on a flight out of Frankfurt returning to the States from Asia, I was seated next to an obviously wiped-out, middle-aged businessman. He sat silently slumped in his seat until the plane took off. Not until the cabin attendant served us dinner and a drink did he say a word.

"Lagos," the man finally mumbled, catching my attention. "I was in Lagos." I replied that I knew Lagos. He went on. "I just had the scare of my life there." He explained that he sold telecommunications equipment and that his Texas-based company had been contacted by a Nigerian official who said the Nigerian government wished to buy their equipment. "So I flew to Lagos," he said. "The general who had issued the request personally met me at the airport. Then, after arrival at the fortresslike Sheraton Hotel, the scene changed. I was told my company was out of the running and that I was in the country illegally. He told me I couldn't leave and that I might be jailed."

The Texan continued his tale of Nigerian woe. After being held in the hotel for five days, scared to death every second, the general asked how much money he had with him, hinting that a deal could be worked out. Otherwise, it was off to jail. The Texan gave him every red cent he had on him, fifteen thousand dollars in cash and travelers checks. Immediately he was taken to the airport and put on the plane. Unfortunately, this was very typical of doing business in Nigeria. I expressed my sympathy.

"What are you going to do when we land in Washington?" I asked. "Do you have any money at all?"

"I don't know, and I don't have a dime," he said. "I'm so relieved to be out of Nigeria that I can't think about it."

Knowing he'd need cash, I gave him a hundred dollars. "I've been there. If that had happened to me, I'd need some money that I wouldn't want to ask for."

Three days later, in Virginia, I received a check and a thank you note from the man. Just another routine Nigeria story.

The Lagos shakedown took many forms, and the Texan had just experienced one of the ruses that typify the lawlessness that exists in Nigeria. I was increasingly to discover that the law of the land, at least the way we understand it, was no law at all.

Nigeria is also infamous worldwide for the well-known bank scam that claims to pay someone 10 percent of $27 million, just for letting some hush-hush Nigerian government money be washed through their bank account. The scam has been going one for more than twenty years and is a perfect example of what the country is like.

After the episode with the Texan, I was less than thrilled to be returning to Nigeria. I'd just returned from Tokyo when I received a telegram regarding a contractual problem in Nigeria. Before I knew it, I had a ticket and visa and was on my way back to wonderful Lagos.

I landed at midday for a change. I sat around a safe transit house for two hours as my driver, sent by the institute I was to see, lounged. We left in late afternoon for the two-hour drive to Ibadan, a hilly, forested city of roughly three million, located due north of Lagos. The institute's vehicles were clearly marked. Local bandits knew they carried educators and agriculturists so, generally, they were not targets on the open stretch of highway. That was during daylight. After dark, everyone was fair game.

The ride was uneventful until the sun started to set. Unexpectedly, the driver put the gas pedal to the floor. The car accelerated to ninety miles per hour, an extremely dangerous speed given both the road conditions and the dilapidated state of the car. I advised him to slow down. "When the sun goes down," he said, "robbers take over the road."

"So why didn't we leave earlier?" I asked. The driver merely shrugged as he increased speed to one hundred miles per hour. If we'd had a tire blow out, we'd have surely died in a horrible accident. It was easily the most frightening car ride of my life.

Just like the damn Masai guide, the driver had given no apparent thought to the consequences, the absolute guaranteed outcome, of leaving so late in the day. His logic was mired somewhere in a cultural "no man's land" about which most Westerners have no concept. It was so similar to the hippo guide, yet the religious and tribal cultural differences probably spanned an area best measured in light years. I was struck by the similarity even as I held on to the shaking, rattling car for dear life.

Understanding an absence of logic seemed to me like an oxymoron, yet it was precisely what I needed to do. I decided I would ask a variety of questions whenever being led or directed by a local—I would not blindly assume consequences had been weighed. Without being irritating, I would try to probe the whys, whens, and hows deeply enough to shed any illumination possible on potential culturally rooted logical differences. By doing so, I would be able to better avoid potentially dangerous situations.

It developed there was a misunderstanding with the institute—not a contractual problem. You can imagine how pleased I was to find that out, knowing I still had the return ride to Lagos and the semiofficial mugging at the airport ahead of me. Once again, I was confronted with success by no other factor than showing up.

Cultural Snapshot

While in Ibadan, I was sitting outside having a beer. Just at sundown, the nightly migration of the fruit bats began as they moved from their daylight sleeping locations to the fruit trees. The bats darkened the sky like a blanket of heavy smoke. Eerily and most incredibly, there was not a sound. There were millions of them—millions—from horizon to horizon. A single shot from a pistol would have taken four, maybe even a dozen, bats in flight. It was an awe-inspiring event to witness, the damnedest occurrence of nature I had ever seen. None of the locals seemed to give this unbelievable event a second thought.

Indonesian Bargain:
A Lesson in Leverage

Indonesia became a regular stop due to a complicated project there that was eighteen months in the planning stages.

No story better illustrates the aspects of a simple negotiation than some related incidents that occurred during my visits to Indonesia. On my third trip to Jakarta in a little over a year, I was running a bit late for my flight out. I had learned to leave for the airport with plenty of time to spare as the traffic in Jakarta, at times, came to an absolute standstill.

I checked out at the front desk of the Borabadour Hotel and was headed for the escalator when I decided to take just a second to see if a painting that I had tried to buy more than a year earlier was still in one of the hotel arcade shops. I had by now become quite an art buff, and, in addition, I had a carpet addiction. Whenever possible, I made time to find art made by local artists.

In my first conversation with the owner of the shop, I had offered what I considered a reasonable price for the painting. At five hundred dollars, the price the owner wanted, the painting was very expensive compared to what it would bring in a shop anywhere else in Jakarta. I applied my rug *souk* rule and began the bargaining with an offer of about one-third of the asking price, but the owner would have none of my offer. I suspected he perceived my keen interest and believed he could get his asking price. Instead, I just walked out.

I came back three months later to see if the painting was still there. It was, so again I offered the owner one hundred and fifty dollars. He said he had many people interested in that particular painting, and he expected to sell it very soon for a price even higher than the one at which it was currently offered. I *really* loved the painting and had to have it, but, again, I walked out.

On a third trip, hurriedly peeking into the shop, I was surprised to see the painting. It no longer occupied a prominent spot at the front of the shop, but was resting on the floor toward the rear. The person lounging behind the shop counter was not the owner I had haggled with in previous trips. I asked if the painting was still for sale, and he said it was. I realized the owner had tried to sucker me the last time and probably had never acquired another offer on the painting.

Instantly, I formulated my negotiation tactic. I asked the man at the counter if the owner was around. He answered "yes" and retreated behind a curtained door. The owner emerged moments later. I could tell from his eyes that the owner remembered me immediately.

I gave him no chance to think. I took one hundred dollars in cash and held it out to him. I announced firmly that I had a plane to catch, and I was in a hurry. I informed him, as he well knew, that the painting I wanted had been in his store for over a year. I put the cash on the counter and declared that I would pay this and no more. Right now!

Both the owner and I understood the leverage had changed. The owner's dishonest negotiation tactic was exposed. Not only had I initially established leverage by walking away, I had achieved significant leverage by the exposure of his deceitful bargaining. Most importantly, the owner knew that *I knew* all this.

The owner also knew I would *never* pay five hundred dollars, not now. By using the only real leverage I possessed over the year, that of walking away, I was able to capture, by a combination of luck and tactics, an even greater degree of leverage.

Without a word, the store owner began to pry the painting from its wooden frame. Within a minute, he had it neatly rolled and placed into a round protective container I could easily carry onto the plane. I left, in possession of the painting, no more than five minutes after I had walked in.

While this negotiation occurred in Indonesia, the essential elements to the incident could have played out anywhere in the world, including the United States. The important aspect of this story is the perception of leverage. For leverage to be exercised, both parties must perceive the same leverage. By the same token, the misperception of leverage can result in utter defeat.

In a celebratory mood, I headed for my flight to Europe en route back to the United States. By the end of the 1980s, traveling into and out of Europe had taken on an entirely new dimension. The bombing of Pan Am Flight 103 over Lockerbie, Scotland before Christmas 1988 brought security to a very heightened level at airports. Every European airport began a new security process, with Frankfurt being exceptionally diligent. The Germans were not at all pleased at having been caught napping in the Pan Am bombing.

All flights destined for the United States were encircled on the tarmac by the checked luggage to be pointed out by the boarding passenger. Only after being identified by the passenger on the tarmac, with the passenger then immediately boarding, was the baggage loaded. The new process was designed to prevent any piece of baggage from being loaded onto a flight that wasn't the property of a passenger. This screening process went on through rain, sleet, snow, or bone-chilling cold. It was easily the most onerous and time-consuming of the new security procedures. Many times during the next three to four years, I was on planes held up on the tarmac for hours when the checked baggage was not fully identified on the tarmac. Twice, planes I was taking were emptied and reboarded.

Passenger screening jumped to a whole new level as well with an interview that consisted mainly of questions regarding your background and journey and took place while your passport was carefully examined.

Those of us who witnessed the changes in Europe knew what was in store in the United States after the September 11 tragedy. The effects of September 11 continue to dramatically affect the travel environment worldwide, even years later.

Sign of the Times

The passport scrutiny at the airport check-in was the part of travel that became so very cumbersome for me. My passport was easily an inch thick, containing stamped visas from just about every perceived terrorist spot in the world. I was inevitably asked to step out of line and detained until the chief security officer could be summoned to interview me. I became so accustomed to this that I would approach the security area, open my passport and say, "You're gonna want to call the head guy." For a full two years after the Pan Am Lockerbie tragedy, I never got on an international flight where I wasn't interviewed by the chief security officer.

Zimbabwe Smuggling:
Going Straight to the Source

In late 1989 my company won a U.S. government bid for warehousing and shipping services of contraceptives. The United States gives hundreds of millions of dollars a year for world population control, primarily aimed at underdeveloped countries. The materials to be shipped under the contract included condoms, IUDs, birth control pills, and contraceptive patches. By far and away, the main staple of this program was the supply of condoms. Gazillions of them were shipped to practically every country in the world, over one hundred, approved to receive assistance from the U.S. government.

During the three month implementation period we were meeting regularly with U.S. government representatives to discuss past operational problems. One of the interesting problems that arose was a theft issue concerning condom shipments to Zimbabwe. Apparently, a condom smuggling ring was stealing the condoms for resale. Each shipping container held approximately one million condoms, so the smugglers were making tens of thousands of dollars. I believe this absolutely proves the old adage that there is money to be made in everything—you just have to find the angle.

This smuggling issue was such a major problem that I decided to go to Zimbabwe to investigate the problem and, hopefully, solve it. So, off I went to Harare, the capital and largest city in Zimbabwe, to bring a halt to the nefarious condom smuggling ring. Believe me; I more than realize this is a great set-up for a James Bond spoof.

We were all a little embarrassed in the beginning to be talking so openly and clinically about condoms and the other birth control devices. Though that soon wore off, the reactions of the uninitiated were constant. First, the wide-eyed incredulity that there were that many condoms in the whole world, then the *"huh?"* reaction when the smuggling ring was mentioned, followed almost immediately by the slow smirk. The jokes and puns that inevitably followed were the last stage.

So, I arrived in Harare, which reminded me of Nairobi although not as big. Downtown was a smaller, defined area that consisted of a hotel, a bank, and a number of trinket shops.

I had been fully authorized—if not exactly licensed—by the U.S. government to bring a halt to the condom smuggling. I did not bring any weapons, so I wasn't sure how I would stop the smuggling or, for that matter, exactly what I was going to do. Fortunately, I did not run into these obviously hardened criminals.

I went immediately to the warehouse where the condom shipments arrived from Durban, South Africa, the closest ocean port to Harare. If I could not solve the theft issue in Harare, I knew Durban would have to be my next stop.

The manager of the facility in Harare where the condoms were stored was, as luck would have it, a very attractive lady. Her name was Cherith. She was in her midthirties with auburn hair, a great figure, and knockout smile. I was petrified that I would inadvertently use a double entendre and spent most of the meeting praying that I wouldn't. We both blushed from time to time, especially whenever the conversation edged toward the unspoken motivation, as we discussed the theft problem. Incredibly, she had not been aware of the theft problem. It was evident from my cursory investigation that the thievery was occurring prior to reaching the warehouse in Harare.

The source of the problem was evident quickly. As Cherith explained the normal procedures, I was stunned to learn that the shipping process being utilized was archaic, and contrary to standard modern methodology. The boxes of condoms were being unloaded from the sealed, steel ocean containers at the port of Durban and then loaded onto open bed trucks for the transit to Harare. This meant the theft could be at the port in Durban or anywhere in between, most likely during customs clearance at the border of South Africa and Zimbabwe.

I have to say I felt I must have been missing something. It was my understanding that the condom stealing had been an issue for years and many tens of thousands of dollars in losses had occurred. The more I thought about it, I realized my analysis was spot on. The *only* change necessary was to do what should have been done in the first place—keep the condoms in the ocean container and not unload them in Durban. Not only did this stop all the theft, but it was *cheaper.*

The solution here was so obvious, so rudimentary that anyone could have posed it. It was, to me, not unlike solving a problem with getting wet by coming in from the rain—anyone with a double digit IQ could have come up with the solution.

The situations at the hospital in Saudi Arabia and with the institute in Lagos came flooding back to me. All I had done, really, was to show up. I had to have been the only person to have ever investigated this at the source. No James Bond spying, no deep investigation, just five minutes at the source of the problem. The obvious solution was clearly not so obvious from a distance.

I thought of Woody Allen's saying that 80 percent of success was showing up. I had to conclude that Woody had underestimated. It certainly seemed a percent somewhat higher—say ninety at least—would be more appropriate. Nothing is more revealing in solving a problem than being at the source. A very simple rule that, if followed, can yield amazingly good results.

Winds of War:
A Lesson in Remaining Inconspicuous

In August 1990, I was transiting in Paris from Charles De Gaulle Airport to Orly Airport, and I happened to catch a news report on a French channel. I was able to decipher some of the content, mostly from the pictures, having something to do with an invasion of Kuwait by Iraq. Absurd, I thought, countries don't *invade* other countries anymore. Anyway, at the time I dismissed the news report with little to no thought as I flew on to Islamabad, Pakistan.

The landing in Islamabad spoke volumes about the changing tides in the Afghan war with the Soviets. As the announcement to prepare for landing came through the cabin in Urdu, French, and finally English, the 747 banked sharply and began to descend. It was soon apparent that the plane had not turned to reposition but was banking in a controlled tight pattern. Essentially, this huge aircraft was corkscrewing downward in a maneuver I had never experienced before. I don't mean a slightly banked, wide circle—no sir—I mean it felt like a carnival ride. The down wing seemed to make a circle in the air about three feet wide.

As the centrifugal forces pressed me more deeply into the seat, my concern was evidently written all over my face. The gentleman seated next to me offered that the fighting in Afghanistan had resulted in the abundant proliferation of hand-held surface-to-air missiles (SAMs) called Stingers. The United States had flooded the area with so many Stingers that authorities were concerned that one might be fired at a passenger aircraft making a normal landing approach. It was an unintended consequence of the weapons deliveries made legendary by the book and movie *Charlie Wilson's War*. This corkscrew maneuver had become routine for landings because of this.

During dinner with a client that evening, the conversation turned to world events. The client asked if I knew anything about the invasion of Kuwait. It was absolutely the first I'd even thought about the odd news report I had seen in Paris. I explained what I had seen and that I had dismissed it as the typical over-hyped journalism I'd experienced before. I was quickly brought up to speed on the incredible events taking place not far to our west.

The telephone rang with more world news but this time it was literally right next to us. My client returned to the dinner table and told us the caller relayed that a coup had removed Benazir Bhutto, the Pakistani Prime Minister, from power.

We were all concerned. Political coups in this part of the world could get nasty very quickly. My client suggested we go up on the roof of his house to see if we could position his satellite dish to pick up the new twenty-four hour news station, CNN. Against the backdrop of the unusually quiet city, with a sweep of stars against a black sky, we fiddled with the antenna until his wife shouted up to us, "There's a weak signal now!"

In the living room we watched CNN. Through a snowy picture we could make out bits and pieces of the worldwide hand wringing going on about Iraq. Finally, the announcer confirmed that Bhutto had been removed from office in what *appeared* to be a peaceful coup. At the time, the Kuwait situation seemed trivial.

After dinner, en route to my hotel, I saw a distinct deployment of military troops, a sight I'd not seen earlier that evening. I realized I had flown smack into the middle of a couple of touchy world events. Unlike my times in Sri Lanka or Burma, I seemed to be in the middle of the instigating events, and that wasn't good.

The next day I was traveling to India—Bombay to be precise. To reach Bombay from Islamabad without losing three days waiting, I had to route through Karachi and then Muscat, Oman. Changing planes in Karachi, I exited the domestic terminal en route to the international terminal and became immediately aware of a very loud, apparently very large disturbance. It took only a moment to realize it was a demonstration in progress, and, from what I could instantly assess, it was a virulently anti-American one.

Oh boy, I thought, *if it weren't for bad luck on this trip, I wouldn't have any luck at all!* There had to be thousands of people—the sound was like being in a crowded raucous sports stadium. I couldn't help but think just how pleased they might be to come across a real live American. Yep, I was feeling pretty darn unlucky.

I immediately became aware of my appearance. I certainly didn't look Pakistani, but at least I didn't look stereotypically American. I was dressed distinctly un-American, and I even had on those fashion faux pas white socks. I could easily pass for Dutch or German. This was exactly the type of situation that made my precautions worthwhile. My now habitual efforts to be as inconspicuous and un-American looking as possible certainly buoyed my confidence as I strode purposefully and without being accosted to the international terminal.

The demonstration I had stumbled into at the Karachi airport was a harbinger of the mass demonstrations to be held throughout the Middle East over the next few months. The anti-Americanism that fomented due to the war to liberate Kuwait was so widespread that I would not travel outside the United States until after the end of the war.

Sign of the Times

Landing in Oman, I was witness to a goosebump-raising sight. My plane was held unaccountably on the tarmac, and I spotted incoming aircraft from my window. Over the next half hour I watched approximately thirty camouflaged C-130 cargo planes land in turn, one after another, in rapid succession.

After finally deplaning, I learned in the terminal that I had just watched the first British Royal Air Force troop deployment into the Persian Gulf. Oman, I was told, was a British area of protection, and these were the first troops arriving in the buildup to the Gulf War. For the first time I realized the invasion of Kuwait was serious, really serious.

It's Greek to Me:
Lessons in Maintaining Face
on a Macroscopic Scale

The Gulf War ended in a mere matter of months, but the anti-Americanism raging throughout the world would keep me off the road for over nine months—the longest period I had gone without traveling outside the United States in ten years. Within weeks of the end of hostilities, I took one of the first flights into war-ravaged Kuwait, connecting out of Cairo. The flight lasted a little over two hours. Only a short time into the flight, and probably still a thousand miles away, I was stunned to see a pall of smoke from the seven-hundred-odd burning oil rigs already extending across the horizon. As we descended to land at Kuwait City, the plane dropped below the thick blanket of smoke. Dotting the ground were hundreds of plumes of fire, some flames as high as eighty stories rising straight up in the air. The Iraqis had certainly created a disaster!

As we landed, it was immediately obvious that the airport had been a battleground. Trenches had been dug and sandbagged between runways. Remnants of weapons and other debris of fighting could be seen lying around. As we deplaned, I saw that the terminal had been shot up pretty bad. A gaping hole marked the roof, and bullet holes everywhere. The hole in the roof meant no air conditioning, and it was June. So, of course, it was hot as hell.

I checked into what was then Le Meridien Hotel, and was perhaps the most extensively damaged building in the city. One of the waitresses in the hotel restaurant told me that an Iraqi tank pulled up one day shortly after the occupation and, solely for the amusement of the Iraqi troops, started shelling the lobby and floors above. For the locals unable to flee, the occupation went pretty much like that.

The cab driver who brought me in from the airport had told me that I must see the "Highway of Death," referring to the road leading north from Kuwait City toward the Iraqi city of Basra. The following day, I hired a guide of sorts to take me out to see the famed highway.

The driver/guide explained to me what had occurred and what he had personally witnessed. As the American advance had come upon Kuwait City so quickly, the Iraqi troops commandeered thousands of vehicles—cars of every make and model, jeeps, VW vans, trucks of every size and shape, and school buses by the dozens—trying to make their hurried escape out of Kuwait City. The carnage in front of me was a testament to the fact that they waited too long.

The fleeing vehicles, all crammed full of Iraqi troops, stretched some ten miles from Kuwait City toward Basra. U.S. Apache helicopters, dozens of them, had hovered half a mile or so away from the road and unleashed their deadly weaponry. As one Apache spent its weapons payload, it was replaced in position by another fully armed one. According to my driver, this went on for hours. The carnage that occurred right where I was standing left quite an impression, and I reflected upon it for some time.

Soon afterward, I went to Greece to meet with a new Athens agent to verify and investigate puzzling instructions we had been given regarding a U.S. government program for its famous broadcast entity, the Voice of America (VOA). I say "puzzling" because from the looks of the instructions, for all practical purposes, my company was being asked to sneak communications equipment and a broadcasting tower into Greece. Yep, that's right. Sneak it in.

The equipment was for an expansion and modernization of an existing relay station that first began broadcasting in 1964 from the Greek island of Rhodes. Rhodes is typical of the Greek tourism posters with idyllic, white-washed villas hugging a deep, blue-hued beachfront. The most eastern of the Greek islands, it sits just miles from the Turkish coast, almost directly south of the city of Izmir. The location is perfect for broadcasting uncensored news into the Middle East and Northeast Africa, regions well known for limited free speech and government-censored information.

The agent I was meeting was an American who had been living in Greece for twenty-some years by virtue of his marriage to a Greek woman. The agent, Jim, was slender and perhaps fifty years of age. He had been involved with the U.S. embassy previously on shipping programs of "priority," as he called them. During dinner, at a great little restaurant in a seaside resort area just outside of Athens, I got the distinct feeling he was pretty wired into both the local Greek and American communities. Jim explained to me the political issues involved with the Greek government allowing Voice of America [VOA] to operate this broadcasting station, and the unusual arrangement began to make sense.

The political relationship between Greece and the United States was a complicated one. Issues regarding its traditional enemies Turkey, the Balkans, and Israel were major components of the much broader international context that affected U.S.-Greek relations. With this greater international context in mind, sensitive issues tended to evolve in the direction of least resistance.

Evidently, some political rub had evolved between the U.S. and Greek governments having to do with the status of the relay station in Greece. Essentially, the VOA station had never received Greek approval to exist. Since the relay station did, in fact, exist, modernizing it was seen as a technicality best undertaken as quietly as possible. Public knowledge of the modernization efforts would put the Greek government in an embarrassing predicament.

The equipment was to be sent completely unmarked and described only as government cargo to the U.S. embassy. The U.S. embassy would bring the equipment into Greece under its diplomatic status and then turn the equipment over to our agent. The modernization equipment was then to be quietly transported to the deserted area of Rhodes where the relay station was located.

As I processed this information, my experience with Murki flashed through my consciousness. Like a revelation, I was certain of the forces at work in this situation. This was the first time I had become intertwined in a macroscopic "political" situation of saving face. It was incredible that the importance of saving face could spur this kind of government to government "wink."

My experience with the Greek situation was the impetus to a conclusion that I drew regarding the termination of the Kuwait war. I was sure the devastating scene I had witnessed on the Highway of Death must have been repeated throughout the war theater. The slaughter, if it continued, and certainly if it was duplicated or surpassed on other battlegrounds, would have undoubtedly become a touchy subject, resulting in shame and embarrassment throughout the entire Arab world.

I believe a major consideration regarding the end of that war was that of saving face. Years later, the problems encountered in the aftermath of the Iraq war led to other theories regarding the premature end of the Kuwait war—primarily dealing with the broad insurgency. Hindsight is twenty-twenty, and I just don't think those theories were in play after the Kuwait war. No, I believe that concerns revolving around saving face not just for the Iraqis but also for the entire Arab World were very probably discussed among President Bush, General Schwarzkopf, General Powell, and Secretary Cheney. I believe the war had been terminated and the carnage I witnessed kept as quiet as possible due to those concerns. In a "macro" global context, it was, at its crux, an issue of saving face.

Sign of the Times

The Highway of Death was a scene that only those who have ever seen the aftermath of war can truly understand. Pictures in books are a poor substitute for revealing the full impact. I was overcome with a profound sense of the awesome power that had been unleashed there. My father landed at Utah Beach during D-Day, and he once told me that he felt he couldn't adequately describe what he had experienced. I felt that I now understood what he meant, as words fail me in adequately depicting what I witnessed.

The twisted wreckage that once had been vehicles lay scattered in heaps and piles, along both sides of the road, as far as I could see to the horizon. Occasionally there was a truck or other large vehicle upside down, or on its nose, fifty to one hundred yards off the road. From the obviously destroyed and crumpled remains, it was clear, to even the untrained eye of a noncombatant, that some almost unfathomable force had first obliterated the vehicle and simultaneously propelled it dozens, even hundreds, of yards to its final resting place.

There was unspent ordnance everywhere: tank rounds, machine gun ammunition, rifle casings, scattered so that not one square foot anywhere off the road was barren. Upon closer inspection of the debris I saw boots, shreds of clothing, and spattered blood everywhere. It must have taken weeks to clear the thousands of bodies that without question had met their demise right where I had stood.

The Accidental Thai:
A Lesson in the Law of the Land

In late 1990, a project began in Thailand, and I was back and forth to Bangkok several times within the period of a year. Here I should give a little background. If ever a destination in the world surpassed its reputation, it was Bangkok.

Bangkok is almost impossible to describe adequately to anyone who has not experienced it. The greatest intangible, but the one that permeates every aspect of the city, is the atmosphere. Bangkok is, at a glance, simply a crowded Asian city with warm temperatures and heavy humidity. Transforming the city are the people. This is not a Christian culture, and there is no sense of guilt as we understand it. There is a casual acceptance, something more than simple tolerance, of outsiders or pleasure seekers.

Bangkok is world-renowned for places like the Nana Plaza or Pat Pong, the epicenters for topless dance clubs and sex shows. During the day the areas looks like any slightly seedy area in most any part of Asia. At night, they are transformed into a scene that simply exists nowhere else in the world.

On this trip, I had immediately connected through Bangkok for a flight to Udorn, the Vietnam-era U.S. outpost. Our agent in Thailand, Ron, a friend for over ten years, met me on the flight. On the trip, I met two real characters, who exemplified the quirky range of Americans drawn to this Asian paradise, and learned a valuable lesson in jurisprudence.

The first American I met was called Fred. He practiced an odd style of conversation that was instantly recognizable, if a bit disconcerting—he repeated the last three words of the person with whom he was conversing. Added to this unique speech pattern was his predilection for speaking in a deep faux-Bogart inflection. It was impossible not to get a little tickled by this pseudo–secret agent speech pattern.

From Ron, I learned that Fred had recently offered a motorcycle as a dowry to marry a local Thai lovely. The nuptials were unexpectedly scrapped when the father, to whom the dowry offering was given, reported the motorcycle stolen the day before the wedding. So much for true love.

Only days later, the father was seen dashing around town on a motorcycle remarkably similar to the one reported stolen. Local legend had it that every month or so a foreigner, usually American, was the patsy in this Thai "marriage" ritual.

One night in Udorn, we attended a local Thai nightclub where Fred's latest love interest was a singer. I use the term "singer" loosely, as her singing sounded like someone killing a cat, and I couldn't help but wonder what the quid pro quo was for this relationship. Singing lessons would have been a good start. It was in this club that I met George.

George was the stereotypical American in Thailand, the kind of guy who never grew out of his college fraternity party mode. He was single in a single man's paradise, and his motto was pedal-to-the-metal partying every night. In a way, it was hard not to be a little envious of George's lifestyle and approach to life.

This meeting carried no significance other than some disturbing news I learned on a later trip to Thailand. A tragic and telling event had put an end to George's carefree days in Thailand, and it gives a provocative insight to an overseas legal system.

Late one night, George had been driving home after an evening of hard drinking and partying. En route, he accidentally struck an elderly woman on a bicycle. Evidently, George was speeding, and the woman was mortally injured. George was in big trouble. If he was convicted, which he would most assuredly be, George could spend years, if not life, in a Thai prison.

However, George had learned more than how to live a life of leisure during his stay in Thailand. He had befriended many important locals and had become familiar with the ways of the local judicial system. George hired an influential Thai lawyer that carefully concocted a ruse that Fred's would-be father-in-law would have admired. To guarantee George's freedom, another person stood trial in his place.

To accomplish this ruse a poor local family was approached with a deal. For approximately ten thousand dollars of George's money, the poor family would have one of their sons come forward and testify as being the driver of the car that killed the woman.

Within a matter of days, a deal was struck. With the charges now brought against the son of the poor local family, George immediately fled Thailand back to the States. I believe the young son of that family is still in a Thai prison to this day.

In comparison to Rod's Hajji experience and the Texan's Nigerian escapade, I realized how different those legal situations were to George's. George obviously had taken the time to understand the nuances of the legal system in Thailand. He surely didn't deserve the good fortune of getting away with no punishment, but then Rod and the Texan certainly hadn't deserved the consequences that befell them. George was in the wrong, yet he manipulated the system to his favor, while the other two were at no fault and got hammered by legal systems of which they knew nothing.

It dawned on me that the real legal system in any country could not be assumed to bear any resemblance to that of the United States or any other Western culture. Further, I realized that one must understand the law of the land.

Cultural Snapshot

Areas like Pat Pong in Bangkok are unlike any other in the world. One enters Pat Pong under an Oriental style archway and is immediately besieged in a wild setting where the peddlers sell knock-offs of every conceivable item. Name something, and you will find it there for a fraction of the price of the real deal. Purses, luggage, watches, pens, shirts, jackets, and souvenirs of every kind—some quite unimaginable—are sold.

Extending perhaps one hundred yards along the main avenue, jammed into every square foot possible between the clubs lining both sides of the narrow street, are people just like your mom and dad, your Aunt Mary and Uncle Ned, or even the pastor from your local church. Buses filled with these folks, just back from touring one of the many magnificent, gold-plated palaces or Buddhist shrines, unload at one end of the area, spilling tourists into this incredible den of iniquity.

Beautiful young women stand casually about outside every club, available to anyone who strikes the right deal with the mama-san standing guard. It's mind boggling. Tourists of all ages, from nearly every country, can be seen along with business people, college kids, and transvestites. Even so, it is, for all intents and purposes, a very safe place to be.

Iron Curtain Culture:
A Lesson in Historical Context

My company had reached its sixth year and had grown so rapidly that, in 1991, we were ranked eighty-fourth of *INC Magazine's* five hundred fastest-growing U.S. companies. Our revenues had multiplied over 2,000 percent from our first year of operation to our fifth year. As impressive as this growth was, it was still only the beginning—especially as new markets emerged with the fall of the Iron Curtain.

The fall of the Soviet puppet states in Eastern Europe were symbolized for the world in late 1989 when the Berlin Wall was torn down. I was in Paris when the massive celebrations began in Berlin and tried in vain to travel there to soak in the historic occasion, not to mention absconding with a piece of the Wall. Not only were flights booked heavily, the major problem was getting a hotel room—even the youth hostels were overbooked.

I watched the unfolding events in Eastern Europe with the sense that a tremendous business opportunity was about to unfold. In early 1991, my first chance to get a peek behind the now defunct Iron Curtain arose. A year and a half after that night in Paris, I was going to get my first look at two of the former Iron Curtain countries, Hungary and Bulgaria.

My initial stop was Budapest. I was very surprised by the generally positive living conditions. Hungary had been among the most open of the Soviet bloc countries for years, and it showed. The center of Budapest, with its many cobblestone streets and eighteenth-century architecture, looked very much like sections of Vienna or Zurich or any of the other classic western European cities. Good hotels were plentiful; there were well-appointed restaurants; and the city center shops were well stocked. My impressions of Budapest made me think the news reports of the dire circumstances of life in Eastern Europe were overblown. I soon realized how wrong I was.

As I continued on to Sofia, Bulgaria, I saw absolutely deplorable living conditions. There were lines of people seeking food and clothing, dirty unkempt streets, and evidence of the watchful eye of "Big Brother" everywhere. My experiences in both places struck me as tremendously revealing about the cultural foundations that had developed in these disparate, though politically linked, cities.

In Budapest I sought the help of a local Hungarian, Dmitri, who worked at the U.S. Embassy. We had dinner in a wonderful little café in the suburbs of Pesht, on the west side of the Danube River, which, combined with Buda on the east side, make up Budapest. I was fascinated by life under the Soviet occupation, and I pumped him with questions.

Dmitri's English was very good, and I wondered how he had been able to learn the language. Dmitri explained that English hadn't been taught in his Hungarian school and having any knowledge of it attracted suspicion and scrutiny. Most Hungarian families taught English to their children at home. In Dmitri's case, his grandmother had taken particular interest in his instruction.

I inquired about Dmitri's Russian, and he said it was terrible. Surprised by this, I asked how that was possible. Dmitri explained that the best possible rebellion at school was to get an A in every subject and an F in Russian. Flunking Russian became a badge of honor, highlighting a quiet, yet clear, rebellion.

I asked if teachers or other state officials ever gave retribution for this sort of rebellion. He replied that yes, it was a big deal. His parents were called to the school, and they pretended to be upset. At home, his mother and father couldn't have been more proud. His grandmother was so proud she came to tears every time he was called to the carpet for flunking Russian.

With this moving dinner only days behind me, I visited an old church in Sofia, Bulgaria that had survived the half-century of Soviet occupation. The Alexander Nevski Cathedral, a beautiful structure, so out of place with its surroundings, is famous to this day for its collection of antique religious icons. I went to the cathedral on a souvenir hunt and emerged with an experience far more lasting.

Entering the huge, ornate structure, I was approached by a curator. He recited a bit of the history of the Cathedral and of the hundreds of religious icons on display throughout the church. I listened somewhat inattentively. Through the daze of my inattention, I realized the curator had begun to explain that every icon in the church had been hidden during the Soviet occupation and that hundreds of different families had partaken in the deception. I was amazed. There were easily a thousand icons in my immediate view. Continuing on, the curator clarified that harboring icons had been punishable by death and that many families who were discovered harboring the banned icons were executed.

That so many families had been prepared to pay the ultimate price for rebellion was a deeply inspiring realization. Dmitri's story and the pride of his grandmother came immediately to mind. There were thousands more like her in Bulgaria, and I was certain many thousands more throughout the countries behind the Iron Curtain. Seen in a cultural light, the fall of the Soviet Union had been inevitable.

Such was my introduction to the former Soviet puppet states. It was a revealing and important first cultural look at a part of the world in which I was soon to become immersed.

To Russia with Love:
A Lesson in Communist Corporate Culture

I had watched the collapse of the Iron Curtain across Europe with a sense that the Soviet Union could not be far behind. Immediately after the collapse of the "Evil Empire," I made up my mind that I'd be traveling there at the first opportunity.

For years, I had realized that the Soviet Union represented a major business frontier. I knew that, after the collapse, capitalists would descend upon the enormous virgin territory in droves. Horror stories were coming out of the new republic of Russia—tales of canceled flights, grounded for days or weeks, abominable hotels, currency problems, and rampant crime— all giving a glimpse of what was in store for the business traveler seeking to capitalize on Russia's new open market.

The "new" Russia was one of twelve countries comprising the Newly Independent States (NIS), later called the Commonwealth of Independent States (CIS). I was fairly sure I understood the path that the business development process would follow. Most importantly though, as opposed to my first experience in Saudi Arabia, I possessed a high degree of confidence in my ability to successfully navigate the risky business path that most certainly lay ahead.

My confidence came from my experiences over the last decade. By rough calculation, I had been on the road, actually in a plane or overseas, for almost three of the last ten years. I'd made dozens of trips to nearly sixty countries throughout Europe, Africa, Asia, and the Middle East. Since that first day when I was fleeced by the Saudi cab driver, I had learned vital lessons in how to do business internationally.

Around the time that we prepared to enter Russia, I became very aware of how often I'd been riding by the seat of my pants and that there were times when I had somehow known what the next step or decision needed to be. I often found myself feeling strongly one way or another without any empirical basis for my feelings. I began to keep track of those situations, and, over time, I found my nonempirically led decisions, like the one to forego the Khartoum trip, to be mostly correct. This intuition, or as I preferred to say, "riding by the seat of my pants," became a skill that I worked to develop and recognize.

From the beginning of the NIS gambit, I realized that if I were to going to have any measure of success in this wild and wooly new market, I would have to rely on my intuition.

So it was that in June 1992, as the Boeing 727 ferrying me and dozens of other first time visitors descended through the clouds, I strained to catch my first glimpse of Moscow. Upon landing there, I was filled with a sense of excitement I had not felt since that first landing in Saudi Arabia. The arrivals hall was dark, and the Moscow airport itself, Sheremetyevo II, was not much more modern than the old airport in Cairo. After an interminable delay at immigration, I exited through the customs area into the foreboding-looking crowd.

I had met a gentleman on the flight who worked for the World Bank. We had agreed to share a cab, as we both had heard the horror stories of Westerners being ripped off in airport cabs. If I'd learned anything from my international adventures thus far, I could count on it.

The banker and I settled in for the forty-five minute ride into Moscow. My senses were on full alert. I was fascinated—I was really in *Russia*. Our taxi, a Lada, was comparable to an early 1950s auto in the states. It was a beautiful summer day, and the bright sunlight glaringly illuminated the shortcomings of almost eighty years of Soviet rule.

Approaching the outskirts of Moscow, I was amazed by the number of multi-story, blocky-looking apartment buildings. Few of the building had sidewalks for egresses or even any pavement surrounding them. Leading down to the streets and between the buildings were dirt paths, looking like the cow trails of my Oklahoma childhood. I could well imagine what walking in them during the rain was like. The clearly unadorned nature of the apartment buildings was a style I recognized as so uniquely Soviet. They were decorated by laundry hanging from small balconies and windows everywhere. I felt as if I had entered a time warp and traveled back to the 1930s. It was all so unexpected. *Welcome to the workers' paradise*, I thought.

During my time in Moscow, I was only able to meet one of the five Russian companies I had contacted for meetings. Four of the companies simply did not show up for meetings, nor did they call to cancel. I left Moscow after three days of waiting for meetings that would not happen, having met only one very unimpressive potential agent.

The flight to St. Petersburg was notable for the fact it was the only time I have ever been on a flight loaded with more people than seats. People grimly stood in the aisles, as if they were riding a crowded subway. The whole experience from the time I arrived was surreal, and it was not going to get any better.

I landed at noon and flagged a cab that took me to the Astoria Hotel without incident. I had been told that St. Petersburg was a more refined and beautiful city than Moscow. It was indeed a beautiful city with beguiling architecture. From afar, the disrepair that had been so evident in Moscow didn't seem as striking. At street level, it was a different story. My hotel was a short walk from the Hermitage Museum, famous worldwide for its beautiful architecture, and I was astonished by the extensive cracks evident on the exterior and the rubble piled indiscriminately all over the place.

As in Moscow, my meetings in St. Petersburg were equally disappointing. Again, only one of five companies met as agreed. By this point, I can't say I was surprised. If anything, I was grateful to have seen at least one.

The one meeting in St. Petersburg was with an Austrian-based company. We met at an office across the plaza from the Astoria, just a walk of only a few hundred yards into a beautiful Czarist-era building. I walked up the staircase to the second floor offices and was shown into a huge room. Though it was on the second floor, the ceilings were at least twenty feet high, and the room appeared to be an entire city block long. Through the filtered sunlight shining through the windows, I could barely make out people working at desks at the far end. As people walked about, their footsteps echoed like gunshots on the old wooden floor.

As I waited for the gentleman I was to meet, my expectations were low. In light of what was to follow, not nearly low enough. The man, named Yvgeny, entered the room with a very young, but competent-appearing woman. Earlier that day, I had made arrangements through the hotel for her to translate our meeting. After exchanging awkward pleasantries, I began by explaining the services my company would require and the timely information feedback that was expected. When I finished, I received blank, quizzical looks from both of them. I tried again, this time simplifying my words and the concepts. Still, blank looks. Even the translator was staring at me as if I were speaking in a strange tongue.

Understand that what I was saying was standard Business 101, nothing exotic or out of the ordinary. The look of total incomprehension on both their parts was truly alarming. It appeared that I would have been better off without the translator.

Struggling to find comprehension on their part, I found myself speaking a little louder and with a badly affected Russian accent. It was ridiculous. I felt like a tourist trying to get directions from a clearly non-English-speaking native. I might have left the meeting, placing the inability to communicate effectively squarely on the translator, save for the next turn in the meeting.

Finally, I thought I saw a spark of comprehension in the interpreter's face. That spark promptly led to perhaps a minute of discussion between her and Yvgeny. Afterward, she turned to me, her eyes still full of puzzlement and asked *why* I would require information from Yvgeny's company. *Why?* The ridiculous nature of the inquiry hit me like a hammer.

In that instant, the feelings and thoughts of the last four days in Russia assimilated into one very clear revelation. Nobody, I mean *nobody*, in that colorless, rundown 1930s-era country had any clue about anything even remotely related to the concept of business. It was a cultural abyss every bit as deep as Omar's disaffection for Muffy. In the former Soviet Union, the "mud" seemed to be quicksand. I had not fully appreciated the debilitating effects of decades of Communism. The sense of despair that engulfed me was palpable and crushing. The meeting was a complete waste of time.

I had a lot to think about on that flight back from Russia. My trip had been a total bust. Well, maybe not a total bust if you count the fact that I had learned that any expectation of Western business practices, or even of general conceptual understanding, was complete stupidity. It was probably the lowest moment I had experienced to that point in my business career, but I wasn't giving up, not with the opportunity of a lifetime staring me in the face.

I can't say exactly why this experience was such a watershed regarding my outlook on culture, but it was. Perhaps it was because I realized that if this commercial void, one I had not experienced even in deepest, darkest Africa, existed to such a staggering degree, then who knew what other basic, elementary concepts could be equally nonexistent? This meant that I would have to scrutinize everything in Russia from a cultural standpoint.

With a sense of surety only possible with an understanding of intuitive signals, I was certain that a major opportunity was at hand. Just as if I had suddenly remembered leaving the water, iron, and lights all on, I was cognizant of the unmistakable urgency this sense brought to my actions. Armed with a decade's worth of experience and a profound respect for my own intuition, I propelled my company to a whole new level of profitability in Russia and the other new republics.

Cultural Snapshot

I hold four lasting images of that first visit to Moscow and St. Petersburg. In Moscow, the first strange image was of waist-high grass everywhere—around the apartment buildings and especially in the parks. It looked so eerie to see people, sitting on park benches, barely visible over the unkempt grass.

The second image was of the street disrepair. There were potholes everywhere. I didn't see a single curb that wasn't crumbled and broken. The third image, and somehow the most unsettling, was the absence of color. I don't know when it hit me exactly, but at some point I seemed to be watching a black and white television show, like an old rerun of the Twilight Zone. From clothing to the signs over stores, there was just no color anywhere.

Lastly, on a redemptive note, the midnight sun effect at St. Petersburg's latitude is exquisitely beautiful. It is an unusual but somehow exhilarating sensation to walk outside at three o'clock in the morning into twilight-like dusk.

Milk for Armenia:
A Lesson in Getting It Done

In 1993, an organization called the Fund for Democracy, located in Washington DC, sought a contractor for shipping humanitarian supplies. This was not your typical commercial company. The Fund was a nonprofit organization operating a program on behalf of the State Department's NIS Task Force, headed by former Reagan confidant Richard Armitage.

The Fund had a contract to cover the shipping costs of any group that donated food, medical supplies, and clothing so desperately needed in the nations of the former Soviet Union. Donations poured in from corporations, charities, church groups and individuals, enough to fill thousands of steamship containers. These containers, often thousands a month, needed to be shipped to hundreds of destinations throughout all twelve republics of the NIS

My first meeting with Fund representatives was polite and cordial, yet it wasn't until a few months later that we received a business inquiry from the Fund. When they called it was about a problem with four twenty-foot containers of powdered milk sitting in St. Petersburg, Russia. The Fund wanted to airlift the containers to Yerevan, Armenia, where living conditions were especially terrible at the time. They wanted to know if I thought we could get the milk delivered. I replied, "I think so," with more certainty than I actually felt.

I was not at all confident we could arrange for the airlift. There were no less than three nearly insurmountable problems. I still had not found an agent in Russia that by any definition offered minimally reliable service, and jet fuel was in acute shortage throughout the NIS. As if these two problems weren't enough, the banks in Russia were notoriously slow and corrupt. It could be weeks, if ever, before we could get money into Russia to charter the necessary aircraft. Nothing, I mean *nothing*, happened in Russia without cash, usually U.S. dollars.

With a sense of indifference born out of frustrated desperation, I decided I had nothing to lose by contacting a company called Antramar. I had not contacted this company during my first trip to St. Petersburg, as one of my staff had connected them to a shady European firm of the same name. I didn't like approaching them now, but we were desperate. The time to make hay in Russia and the NIS was passing quickly.

To my surprise we received a quick reply from Antramar's owner. Not only could he hire two Russian-made IL-76 aircraft, each capable of carrying two containers, but they could obtain jet fuel. They also could have the containers of milk in the air within forty-eight hours. To top it all, Antramar's costs and fees were exceedingly reasonable.

Based on this, but having no idea if Antramar could actually do what they promised, I immediately called the Fund. I told them that we had two IL 76s and fuel, and that we could fly to Armenia from St. Petersburg within two days.

The Fund person in charge, Jim, was hesitant to believe me. He said that he had been talking to over a dozen major transport companies all over the United States and Europe. *Not one* could obtain jet fuel in Russia. To be absolutely frank, I was skeptical, too. I wouldn't have bet a plug nickel on the successful outcome of what I was proposing. I knew this was a huge roll of the dice. "You've got the job," Jim finally said. "Don't let me down."

We had the job, and I assumed Antramar would want cash up front. However, we had no means of getting cash into Russia within two days, at least not into a Russian bank, and there were no branches of Western banks there at that time. I was considering putting one of my guys on a plane that night with the cash, as that might be the only answer. While I was struggling with this deal-breaking roadblock, Antramar's owner informed us they would extend credit to my company.

I couldn't believe it. *Nobody* does this. Not in the NIS anyway. It was such a leap of faith on their part that I was immediately worried about where they got the confidence to extend over thirty thousand dollars credit to us, not to mention how they happened to have that kind of cash in dollars. Newspapers in the United States and Europe were filled with stories about the Mafia in Russia and its omnipresence.

Nevertheless, Antramar did exactly as it said and billed us for exactly the quoted fee. We were heroes with the Fund, and this event was a major factor in the award of a large contract. Even though I was almost giddy from the incredible success, worrisome questions remained. How did Antramar get the fuel? Where did the dollars come from? The office was filled with the refrain from one of my favorite movies, *Butch Cassidy and the Sundance Kid,* "Who are those guys?"

Since my experience in Zimbabwe, I had been very conscious of how I approached problem solving. What I realized, in this instance, was that I had to try something—I had to make a decision. When solving problems, there always exists limited and often contradictory information. To me it has always seemed that the greater an opportunity, the more limited, contradictory, negative, or worrisome was the available information to any profitable business outcome, as was the case with Antramar and its ability to successfully obtain the IL-76 air charters.

It would have been easy to do nothing—to be frozen due to the abundance of conflicting information. I learned quickly that when approaching a problem, it's best to simply make a decision and act.

A Date in St. Petersburg:
A Lesson in Miscommunication

The Fund business was our first significant Russian contract and was a harbinger of all that was to come. From the moment we received the Fund contract, everything took place at a whirlwind pace. My second entrepreneurial endeavor, building a company with Western service values within the NIS, had begun and was proceeding at lightning pace. Needless to say, I was preoccupied with the overwhelming problems that operating in Russia and the other newly emerged nations presented. Also, I still couldn't be certain that Antramar was a company we wanted to do business with. Worrisome questions remained.

I began making immediate plans to go meet these mysterious guys from Antramar. It was three months before I had time to fly to St. Petersburg, but the moment I met Sergey Kuzminykh, the older of the two partners, I liked him. Sergey spoke acceptable, though accented English, was about six feet tall with dark hair, forty years old, and had a bearing that commanded respect. His partner, Sergei Vdovin, was about ten years younger and a dead ringer for the famous Russian ballet star, Mikhail Baryshnikov. If these guys were Mafia, then they certainly broke the stereotype.

At our first substantive meeting held in the café of the Hotel Europa, language differences and the misunderstandings that can ensue proved potentially fatal to the new relationship. My past communications lessons proved invaluable in averting this near disaster.

The initial part of the meeting went well, and I learned much about the duo. Sergey and Vdovin had come to know each other during their service in the Soviet merchant marine service. On the water for twenty years, Sergey had become a ship's captain and one of the youngest in the Soviet merchant marine. He became so trusted by Soviet maritime authorities that he was farmed out, earning foreign currency. He sailed regularly on vessels chartered to Greece, Panama, and most of the major flag registries. Vdovin had been Sergey's chief mate on a number of those voyages, and they had become savvy about the world of trade outside of the USSR.

Sergey and Vdovin had only been in business for six months and, in actuality, had done no business to that point. They had experienced multiple bad episodes with Western companies. "They promise us the world," Sergey said. "We either did work for them and were never paid, or the business they talked about did not happen."

Over the latter part of the long business breakfast, I explained to the duo the requirements necessary to begin a business relationship. I explicitly detailed a major requirement that would encompass a sizeable up front effort. This effort comprised the research and compiling of freight rates from St. Petersburg to nearly one hundred cities throughout the NIS. Information like this was exceedingly difficult to collect, and I had expected the conversation to be taxing, but the turn it took was unanticipated.

The conversation then went as follows:

After a moment of silence Sergey asked, "When do you need rates?"

"Set a date," I replied. I knew this research and compilation would take time, and I was trying to be reasonable by first letting them set a time frame. I already had a completion deadline in mind and as long as Sergey's reply was within that deadline then further discussion would be unnecessary. I was surprised when an anguished look came over both their faces.

"Impossible," Sergey said after a moment, hardening his tone. All of the affability and camaraderie that had grown during the morning seemed to evaporate. Then the two Russians shrugged, and Sergey said bitterly, as if they knew our association would come to this, "You ask what we cannot do. What no one could do."

I was confused by the reply. I thought he meant that no one could, or maybe even would, give rates to so many destinations. I wasn't sure what he meant, but I was sure of one thing. The meeting certainly was not going as I had hoped, and I had to have those rates. The many experiences of the past flashed through my mind as I struggled to make sense of this sudden turn of events.

After another silence that passed like days, I finally said, "Sergey, please tell me what you think I said." "Today is Thursday," Sergey replied stonily, "and you just told us you want hundreds of rates by Saturday."

Instantly, I was so relieved. I audibly breathed a sigh and then smiled. "I spoke too fast," I began. "What I said was 'set a date,' not 'Saturday.'" As the miscommunication dawned on the pair, they also broke out in broad smiles. We all had a laugh about the problems of communicating in a second language. The incident became a running joke among the three of us over the coming years. It was a telling lesson in *mis*communications.

The lesson was simple: if in doubt, or if a conversation takes a strange twist, revisit the initial stages or foundation of the dialogue. Ask the other person or persons to explain what they *think* you said. It's a great way to avoid communication pitfalls, in any language and in any environment.

Cultural Snapshot

People being people, the result of the fall of Communism was an explosion of once-prohibited nightlife. During my first visits to St. Petersburg the nightclub scene was simply incredible. I had been to nightclubs all over the world and had enjoyed some wonderful times in many of them. This was unlike anything I had ever experienced before.

The club atop the Europa Hotel was the place to go in St. Petersburg. It attracted the new glitterati of free Russians, ironically the sons and daughters of former government officials and KGB agents who had lived abroad with their families. This crowd of former society elite now hung out side by side with the local Mafia figures. This club and others were like private playpens, very wild but also very friendly. The nightlife flourished on cash—crisp one hundred dollar bills floated about like confetti.

Two for Ceylon:
A Lesson in Delegation

Facing the daunting task of implementing a major contract in Russia with two people I hardly knew, and still harboring residual suspicions that they were part of some type of organized crime outfit, I needed to spend as much time in St. Petersburg as I possibly could. There were dozens of operational details to work out. My schedule wasn't yet clear of one major responsibility that I *had* to undertake before I could truly focus on the NIS. My company was involved in perhaps the biggest Voice of America project yet in Sri Lanka. Both major contractors, Marconi and Brown & Root, wanted us to handle their transport requirements and complicated customs formalities in Sri Lanka.

As I headed off to Sri Lanka, my thoughts revolved around the problem at hand. I was going to the source of the issue, and I knew my information was limited. I was especially worried due to the experiences of my prior trips to Sri Lanka.

Desperate to avoid extra trips to Sri Lanka, I called my Indian friend Willie to ask his advice on agents in Colombo. Willie and I were good friends and possessed identical desires to offer the highest quality services. While I had not been to India in a couple of years, Willie and I always met two or three times a year in Europe or some other nearby area I was visiting, such as Nepal. Often, during our meetings, we would exhaustively explore the business merits of various enterprises and how they could be run better, grown faster, and made more profitable.

Willie didn't know much about the agents in the little country just south of him, but he offered to go down to take a look around He had done just that, and we had then agreed on a date to meet in Sri Lanka. There he would introduce me to the agents he had seen and interviewed.

I arrived in Colombo just after daybreak from Frankfurt. I passed through customs without hassle, grabbing a taxi out front of the small, ramshackle building that was the international airport terminal. I checked into the Hilton about an hour later and took a brief nap. Willie had arranged two days of agent interviews to begin that afternoon.

I met Willie for a late lunch and we left for the first agent meetings. Both were dreadful. That night at dinner, I expressed my worries to Willie. Willie didn't say much, and our conversations turned, as they always did, to dozens of other subjects. In the back of my mind, I was seriously wondering if a competent agent even existed in Sri Lanka.

The following morning we were up early for the first meeting. That agent was worse than either of the two from the prior day. There were only two more meetings that afternoon, and I didn't even have a "lesser of evils" candidate. The fourth meeting was better than all the rest, but still light years away from the aptitude and skills I needed for this project.

Willie had set up the final meeting at the hotel bar. We sat there waiting, and nothing needed to be said. Willie knew we had nothing, and I was concerned. Though Willie had meant well, I was now very much behind the eight ball. Soon we were joined by a representative of a company called Freight Links.

We chatted with the fellow, Niral, for about forty-five minutes before he received a call on his cell phone. He excused himself to take it. My relief must have been written all over my face. Niral's company was exactly what I was looking for. Willie grinned slyly as I told him just that. Willie's smile turned to a broad beam as he explained he had felt the same way, but didn't want to influence my decision. He had intentionally set up Niral for last so I would have all the information I needed to compare to make my decision.

I had been worried whether Willie had done a thorough job, but discovered he had set it up like the absolute pro he was. I should have known from his silence and lack of worry that he had the situation in hand.

Niral returned from his call, and we spent the next two hours setting out expectations and exchanging information. After Niral left, Willie and I went up to dinner. Willie was still enjoying the worry he had seen on my face, and I was giving him a rash of grief for letting me stew. We celebrated at dinner with a couple bottles of the hotel's best wine.

During that dinner, I realized how invaluable Willie's prior research and meetings in Colombo had been. The agent decision, the proverbial chosen path, had been a veritable no-brainer due to Willie's help. Had I not requested his assistance, I could have easily spent many trips, over months of time, resolving this agent issue. Besides going to the source, I had solicited expert help.

In general, the old adage that two heads are better than one is certainly true. My grasp was heightened immeasurably of just how valuable seeking assistance could be when solving problems.

The Assassination:
A Lesson in Being in the
Wrong Place at the Wrong Time

The two days in Colombo in May of 1993 were as intense as I had expected. There were dozens of details to work out to avoid tremendous unexpected costs, which could potentially amount to hundreds of thousands of dollars on a large project such as this. Little did I know that political turmoil was about to strike, yielding the most worrisome, drawn-out escapade of my global travels.

After the second day of meetings, Willie and I, exhausted, prepared to head back to the hotel. The Marconi and Brown & Root people were leaving immediately to visit the VOA project site—a two-hour drive away. We said our good-byes all around, and Niral dropped us off at our hotel.

During the drive to the hotel, the city had seemed oddly quiet. We were winding down from the meetings, and I took no note of it. After a warm farewell to Niral, Willie and I each headed to our rooms to rest before dinner. When I opened my room door, I spotted a small notice slipped under the door. The ominous heading read: "Enforcement of Curfew."

The text announced an immediate curfew declared that afternoon by the government of Sri Lanka. Without explanation, we were warned to stay inside the hotel. I turned the television on only to find a test pattern and solemn music playing on all channels. Something big was up. Having been down this road before, I didn't like the indications. This situation had all the earmarks of the type of civil insurrections I had barely missed in Burma and Somalia. I called Willie, but he knew no more than I. We agreed to meet in the lobby to find out what was going on.

Willie had preceded me to the lobby and looked very somber. He informed me the president of Sri Lanka, Ranasinghe Premadasa, had been assassinated by a suicide bomber that afternoon during the big May Day Parade. The bomber, a suspected Tamil Tiger, had approached the president with a belt of explosives strapped to his waist and detonated it, killing dozens in addition to the president. It had all taken place not a mile from our hotel.

This was not good. Willie and I both knew a little of the history of the decades-long civil war in Sri Lanka. The antagonists were the Sinhalese Buddhists, the majority holding political power for decades, and the Tamil

Muslims, a militant and very violent minority. My first trip to Sri Lanka had been just three weeks after twelve hundred Indian soldiers had been killed while attempting to disarm the Tamils in the north of the island country. The ominous sight of an Indian warship only a few hundred yards off shore during that visit had underscored the tension and undercurrent of violence.

Willie explained that, in retaliation for the Indian government's assistance to Sri Lanka, curbing the Tamil insurgency over the years, a Tamil Tiger had assassinated Indian Prime Minister Rajiv Gandhi two years prior. Hotel employees recounted to us the recent history regarding the large number of assassinations of military officials. Moreover, the Tamils had been waging a campaign of terrorist attacks over the past year that had also killed more than twenty thousand locals. Willie and I returned to our rooms in silence.

Dinner that night was atypically subdued. We were both preoccupied with our own thoughts of the seriousness of the situation.

I vividly recalled being in Pakistan after the outbreak of the Gulf War, having nearly been caught in an anti-American riot at the Karachi airport. Additionally, there had been the Khartoum episode, the Burma situation, and, even more worrisome, a Zaire evacuation of Westerners that I had been intricately involved in from afar.

The Zaire incident—and I knew altogether too much about it for my own good—had disturbing similarities. There the situation caused by rioting soldiers had quickly turned into a major insurrection. More than two hundred and fifty people were killed before French and Belgian troops arrived to help evacuate some twenty thousand foreigners trapped in Kinshasa.

Willie was haunted by the memory of the time he and his wife had been caught in the very rapid, chaotic deterioration in Iran during the overthrow of the Shah of Iran. Willie had been forced to pay substantial bribes for exit visas and airplane seats. In multiple attempts to get out, they had been faced with armed and unruly crowds that created massive riots as the days elapsed. He was certain that the situation in Sri Lanka was going to be far worse than Teheran.

Neither of us voiced our private thoughts that night, and neither of us dared discuss the assassination. It wasn't until many years later that we reflected on the situation and shared our mutual worry over the developing incidents.

As we finished dinner, Willie broke the silence to tell me he would try to get to the airport the next day if the curfew allowed. I agreed wholeheartedly, without stating the obvious. As an Indian citizen, Willie would be in even greater danger than I if Colombo became unraveled.

To say the least, I was very worried about the situation in Colombo. I knew this was potentially a Zaire-type situation brewing. There were no flights to Europe before the one I was booked on two days hence. I reasoned I would just have to cool my heels in the relative safety of the hotel until then. Sleep did not come quickly that night.

The following day Willie was able to book a flight to Bombay and was allowed to travel to the airport. I went out to the hotel car that was to take him to the airport and saw a very decided military presence in the streets. To say a smoldering tension filled the air is an understatement. He promised to call me the moment he reached home—we both knew the unspoken reason.

After Willie left, the day dragged like few others since I'd begun my travels in the mud. To my relief, Willie called that night to assure me he'd arrived safely. My flight was early the following morning, and he insisted that I let him know as soon as I landed in Europe.

My ride the following morning to the airport was uneventful but filled with apprehension. The military was everywhere. Their presence was really not much of a relief and only served to underscore the unpredictability of the situation. As the plane lifted off and gained altitude, I was able to relax for the first time since we had learned about the assassination.

I had much time to reflect during that plane ride. My experiences in Somalia, Burma, and Pakistan had come back to brilliant clarity in my mind. I had missed turmoil in those countries only by providence and lucky timing. Those experiences had all been unheeded warnings of the kind of sudden upheavals so possible in the developing world. This visit to Sri Lanka had not been so lucky.

Since I had been in so many powder-keg regions, most people wouldn't think I'd have been quite so unprepared. But I was. I saw that, just as I should do simple things like checking out the fire exit route in a hotel, I should have a plan to immediately leave a country or area the very instant any type of political or civil strife materialized.

Most relevantly, I realized the mistake I had made by staying that extra day. I should have left with Willie, my own plans be damned. If the situation had been like Zaire, my day delay could have been disastrous.

The Master:
A Lesson in Going with the Flow

Later in May of 1993, I returned to St. Petersburg to follow up on the agreements reached in that first breakfast meeting at the Europa Hotel. That meeting had been notable for establishing Sergey and Vdovin's excellent and rare understanding of business concepts. In the former Soviet Union, only the relatively few Russians who had worked in the West had any idea about basic commercial concepts. In Soviet Russia, evading responsibility, saying nothing, and doing nothing unless ordered was the modus operandi for practically everyone. Luckily, Sergey and Vdovin were not of that typical Soviet thinking.

Sergey, who was both catalyst and "captain" of the enterprise, spoke adequate, though limited English. He was proving himself to be rock-solid and the dominant figure in the partnership with Vdovin. Vdovin spoke much better English, but his grasp of Western expectations was never as acute as Sergey's.

I was pleased to see from the Armenian milk situation that Sergey's bookkeeping was completely on the mark. One of Sergey's duties as a ship's captain had been to manage large sums of money for his crew's wages, for fuel, and for numerous other necessities. He learned early in his career as a captain to be meticulous and to account for every cent. This skill was essential to our business. Most importantly, Sergey did what he said he would do. This I had discovered was the essential, and incredibly simple, main rule of a successful partnership.

I soon found my worries about Sergey and Vdovin's connections to the Mafia were completely unfounded. I discovered, much to my surprise, that Sergey worried about potential Mafia contacts and problems more than I did. He was careful in the extreme to avoid any accidental or incidental Mafia contact.

The first step in our relationship was for Sergey and I to set up a formal partnership. Sergey had the legal documents drawn up for my next trip, and we drove to his lawyer's office to sign them. The lawyer's office was small and, in typical Russian fashion, poorly lit. One of the things I never grew used to was the predilection of most Russians to not use electricity. Consequently, most offices were lit only by whatever light happened to filter through the windows.

The documents that were signed set up a Russian corporation that was called a joint venture company in the Russian legalese of the day. The interesting point about the legalese of the day was that it was essentially Soviet law. This joint venture was established as a local company rather than an international one. This decision involved some arcane vestiges of Soviet law that had the advantage of subjecting the company to less scrutiny, and supposedly less taxes, by the fledgling government. Truthfully, no one knew, so the act was really one of formality.

The most memorable aspect of the documents, copies of which I have to this day, was the way they were bound. After the signing was complete, a secretary came out with a huge needle and thread and sewed the documents together. It seemed somehow very fitting to use such an antiquated binding procedure for an important legal document in this 1930s-era country.

Sergey and I discussed the fact that the vestiges of Soviet law were manifest all over the New Republics and the former Iron Curtain countries. For example, in contrast to Western law, in Soviet law, the stated purpose of the court is to find the "truth" rather than to protect any ideal of legal rights. Sergey explained his own interpretation of Soviet law—that really any particular law was irrelevant. Instead, Soviet law had been set up to enable the courts, or those in power, to reward *or* to convict based upon interpretation. Thus, the "truth" was really at the whim of whoever judged. I knew I needed to be careful.

Early one morning, Sergey and I met to find an office in the city center of St. Petersburg since his current office was well outside of town and not really an office at all. For the volume of business we were about to undertake, real offices with modern equipment were a necessity, so I had requested that Sergey scout downtown areas for an office.

This may seem like an obvious and simple matter, but since the Communists had come to power, there had been no private property in Russia. Under communism, the state owned everything. The properties that interested me no longer had a Soviet ministry running them. No one managed them, and no one owned them. The collapse of the Soviet Union had created macroeconomic and legal problems of monumental proportions. In the ensuing vacuum following the collapse of the Soviet Union, what had evolved was a crazy, upside down Alice-in-Wonderland world—like the one I was about to enter in my simple search for an office.

Sergey had already located a possible space next to the Astoria Hotel in downtown St. Petersburg. The location was ideal—if we could find a way to make a deal. The building itself looked perfectly acceptable, although I was surprised to see a twenty-foot long, eight-foot wide, old wooden boat in the dimly lit foyer. It looked like something in which Washington might have crossed the Delaware. It wasn't in pieces, so I wondered how it got there. I concluded that it must have been built inside the building. It gave the structure a certain nautical flavor, and I thought it a harbinger of good things. Had that been the strangest of occurrences that day, I might have inquired about it, but it wasn't even close.

Standing in the foyer, Sergey told me we were waiting for the building janitor. He was the person to talk to about renting office space. That struck me as strange, but with that boat sitting there in the lobby somehow it wasn't all *that* strange. Within moments, the janitor entered the dank foyer. I had hoped Sergey had used the wrong English word by mistake, but the man was definitely a janitor, and he looked pretty much just like I was afraid he would look.

Sergey and the janitor talked a few short minutes. As they spoke in Russian, I began to like something about the janitor. Sergey turned to me to explain just how it was the janitor could arrange the office rental situation. If I wanted the space, I'd have to pay the janitor for a two-year lease.

Standing there I realized, as hard as it was to fathom, that no one owned this building. Without an owner, any expectation of a lease or any type of rental document was a pipe dream. I realized that this unshaven, unkempt dude before me was the guy I was supposed to pay two years rent, up front, in cash, for the office space we wanted in the heart of St. Petersburg's historic and burgeoning business district. And this was to be done with no legal instrument documenting the transaction. This cash was given in return for a *promise*, from such a dude, that I could rent the offices on the second floor of a building with a *boat* in the foyer. Clearly this was not the typical business school case study.

Sergey lowered his voice and added, "This is the way to go."

I nodded and reached into my pockets giving the janitor the cash. Just like that we had our first office—adjacent to the Astoria Hotel and right across the street from Russia's second most famous cathedral, St. Isaac's. If it were in New York City, it could be compared to having an office on Fifth Avenue across from St. Patrick's, basically, Rockefeller Center.

Walking out with Sergey that day, I chuckled to myself. The situation was absurd but consistent. Sergey saw me smiling and knew what I was thinking. He gestured back toward the building and said, "He is 'Master.'" We both laughed.

Sergey's heavily accented English and style of telling the Master joke had made it my favorite. It went like this:

Two man drivink in car. See green light in front turn red. Driveman give gas and go fast by light. Other man say, "You must stop-ed for red light." Driveman say, "Not need, I am 'Master.'" On drivink two man see red light in front turn green. Driveman slam brake to fast stop-ed. Other man say, "Why you stop-ed like thiz? You master, no?" Driveman say "Yez, I master. But very 'fraid 'nother 'Master' maybe come from other way."

The joke was a parable that succinctly put life in the new republics into perspective by explaining backward Russian logic. Just about every deal and decision over the next four years brought to mind "The Master." Not since the Ensh Allah lesson had a story been so profoundly revealing about the local "logic." Here, everything was indeed backward or upside down. It was my job to turn it right-side up in order to achieve success.

The Cash Capers:
A Lesson in Finance

Conducting business in Russia presented constant and often overwhelming issues. At the forefront of these problems was an odd wrinkle of an age-old problem—that of money. To be more specific, cash. The nature of this problem brought back a memory of an experience at the Jeddah airport in 1984 when I stood in a line behind a Japanese businessman changing dollars into *riyals*. He opened a briefcase, stuffed with packets of one-hundred-dollar bills containing no less than $100,000. I wondered why on Earth he would be coming into the Kingdom with all of that cash. However, in 1993, with business exploding in the old Soviet Union and Sergey's requests for both cash and a formal banking relationship becoming constant, I suddenly understood all that cash carried by the Japanese businessman.

In Russia, besides the fact that no one wanted the local currency, there were no forms of credit whatsoever. There were also no checking accounts, no bank lines of credit, and no credit cards. Everything revolved around cash. Without it, you could do nothing. With it, you could literally move the world.

I *had* to come up with a way to move dollars from Europe directly to Sergey. He simply couldn't operate without cash dollars. Everyone he dealt with had to be paid in U.S. dollars. The use of American cash also had the effect of getting us lower prices and of greatly improving service. Initially, we both doubted that we could keep Sergey stocked with enough cash by flying it in from the States. I needed to figure out a way for Sergey to get U.S. dollars in Europe. What I thought was a fairly simple matter turned out to be anything but simple.

In an effort to solve the problem, I first flew to London, hoping to be able to transfer cash there from the United States. The banks had plenty of British pounds I learned, but they did not keep large stocks of dollars on hand. You couldn't, for example, readily obtain $50,000 in one-hundred-dollar bills. Clearly, London wasn't going to work.

The next solution I tried was to set up an account at the American Express bank in Frankfurt, Germany. We wired money there from our bank, usually in sums in excess of $100,000. The first time we did this, Sergey and I met in Frankfurt for a discussion with the senior bank official.

We found ourselves dealing with a typical German businessman, in this case a *very* traditional banker. He was older and had probably been profoundly impacted by World War II. Germany had fought a desperate war with the Soviet Union, and a portion of Germany in the east had been under the Russian thumb for nearly half a century. Also, during the war, American bombers had pounded the German civilian population. Sergey and I did not represent two of this German's favorite nationalities, and it showed immediately.

This guy knew we wanted dollars. He also knew that the dollars were going into Russia, and he didn't like it. He grilled us minutely about our business, putting questions to us he really had no reason to be asking. We answered him honestly, but we could tell he didn't believe any of it. We were sure he thought we were running drugs. But as much as he displayed his disgust with us, the German had no recourse but to give us the money we requested in dollars.

Leaving the banker's office, I said to Sergey, "I don't know whom he disliked the most, me or you."

"Oh, Ron," said Sergey ruefully. "I am Russian. Given the last fifty years, I think it's me."

The next day, Sergey tucked $60,000 in cash into his blue blazer. We joked as he left that he would own the most expensive sports jacket in Russia.

As we did this again and again, we realized that shuttling the money through the American Express bank in Frankfurt was not just cumbersome but also expensive. Large fees were assessed for the accumulation of dollars. As in London, U.S. dollars weren't that readily available. It seemed the best route for the bulk would be via me and my staff from the United States. We would just have to work at the cash supply and schedule trips based upon both client business and Sergey's cash needs.

On the first trip of the experiment, I brought as much cash as I felt comfortable with. Having said that, the amounts I carried were never comfortable. On that particular trip, I brought $30,000 with me, more than triple the amount I usually carried, yet it was the smallest amount I would carry over the coming years. I had separated the bills into packets when I left and tucked them in my suitcases and my jacket.

Carrying cash like this broke no U.S. laws. We filled out the proper forms when we made the high profile withdrawals from our bank and kept strict inter-company account of the transactions. It was, however, a violation of Russian law when I entered Russia with it and misrepresented the amount on the declaration papers. I'd been warned that if I made large cash declarations the information would be turned over to criminals with whom the customs officials were in cahoots. The misrepresentation was all about avoiding being mugged and robbed. Russia didn't seem all that different from Zaire in that regard.

The Russians, however, weren't stupid. They knew that U.S. dollars were essential for commerce in their country, so they largely turned a blind eye to Western businessmen arriving with bulging coats. Personal searches were quite rare, and, when they did take place, they were not to find hoards of money, but for other reasons.

Trying to retain plausible deniability, I decided to declare to the Russians only a tenth of the cash I actually had on me. The reason I declared one tenth of the sum rather than another percentage was that, in the unlikely event I was searched, I would claim I'd dropped a zero, and then I'd smile at my stupidity and declare the correct amount. This was the system I taught to no less than ten of my staff as we brought cash, hidden in socks, jackets, even panty hose containers, into Russia over the next four years.

On this first cash running trip, I attempted to give the cash to Sergey just after checking into the hotel. My flight had arrived late in the day, and it was almost sundown. Sergey shook his head and asked if I would mind keeping the cash until the next morning. He went on to explain that an old Russian proverb warned of very bad luck from exchanging money at sundown. Given my other overseas sundown experiences with lions in Kenya and robbers in Nigeria, I wasn't going to push the point, although I wasn't at all keen about keeping the money in my hotel room.

The next morning Sergey and I began a routine we were to repeat many, many times in the coming years. He arrived at my room to count and inspect the cash to ensure the bills met the Russian banks' acceptance criteria. First and foremost, one-hundred-dollar bills only. Moreover, no bill could be more than four years old. Any bill that was ripped, soiled, or looked remotely as if it had been washed was not acceptable. Nor was any bill that had been written on.

In order to accommodate the rules under which Sergey had to operate, the two of us would sit down and finger each bill in the stacks that I'd brought. In time, we got very proficient at it. First, I'd check to see if it was the right year and then hand it to him to see if it passed the crispness standard. Out of $30,000, about $4,000 was typically of no use to Sergey, and I carried the flunked money back home.

Over the next few years, this operation of ours resulted in more than a million dollars in cash finding its way into the New Republics.

We had tried a solution, chosen a path, and found over time that it really didn't work. Solving problems is like that. Times change and situations evolve. Solutions also need to evolve. An idea that is a gem of its time can, depending upon the forces of change, quickly become antiquated.

Cultural Snapshot

One of the earliest Western banks to open in St. Petersburg was Credit Lyonnaise, the French- based bank. Shortly after opening its doors, Sergey and I went there to discuss banking and, most importantly, security arrangements. The Mafia was infiltrating banks and then strong-arming their depositors, and I wanted to be sure that could not happen.

Located not far from our offices, the bank resembled a fort—stoic special forces–type guys stood grim-faced outside thick walls. We had to show passport identification to gain access. There were interior partitions which were passable only by showing identification again. Armed SWAT-types were visible everywhere. I found all this very reassuring.

At the interior security access window, an officer positioned behind bulletproof glass asked who we were there to see and phoned to verify our appointment. A machine gun–toting guard escorted us to an elevator. As we stepped into the elevator, he announced in perfect U.S. Midwestern English, "Mr. Putnik will meet you on the fourth floor." I was taken aback. This very same guard had just moments before bid us hello, or at least that was my assumption, and conversed briefly with Sergey in immaculate Russian.

Sergey was as stunned as I. Inside the elevator, I asked Sergey if the guard's Russian had been good. "No" Sergey said. "It was perfect."

I replied that his English was perfect as well. The guard's smooth linguistic skills reminded me of the KGB's infamous "Charm School," written about in a best-selling fiction novel by Nelson DeMille. The Charm School was the place where young Soviet Special Forces types were trained to speak and act with every nuance of Americana. I knew I had just met a graduate of the real Soviet Charm School.

A Kazak View to the Holy Grail:
A Lesson in the Value of Information

I was soon off to Kazakhstan with an eye to opening an office there. The primary reason for the trip was to make arrangements for the shipment of a large mobile medical laboratory by the Merck Company, the pharmaceutical giant that had donated to a charity called BOPEK. The charity was supervised by the wife of Kazakhstan's president, Nursultan Nazarbayev.

Merck had sought us out because of our growing reputation for successful delivery in the former Soviet Union. This delivery was going to be very, very difficult, and not just because it involved a journey longer than from New York to Los Angeles without an interstate highway system.

Kazakhstan was just beginning an economic boom, and the flight down was mobbed. Lufthansa had been operating a Frankfurt-Almaty route for only a month, and reservations proved exceedingly difficult to obtain. The flight packed with businessmen was an encouraging sign, as I've found them an effective barometer of the business environment. I arrived expecting to find fertile ground and was not disappointed.

Almaty was pretty rugged in those days. First, the airport was worse than any I had seen in the Middle East or Africa. The international arrivals terminal was positively prehistoric. It was, really and truly, a hut constructed of stones that had certainly not been built with its present purpose in mind. Rubble was piled inside the building where part of a wall had collapsed.

Dismal as this was, the surroundings were spectacular—high, jagged, snow-capped mountains, the city sited on a steppelike plateau. All very exotic, but everything man-made had that dilapidated, exhausted look common throughout the NIS.

The car sent to meet me dropped me at the Otrar. It was a hotel that resembled an open dormitory, complete with a sour-smelling lobby, filled with disreputable-looking hangers-on. The building was open at both ends, sort of like an old aircraft hanger. You could walk down the hallway and step right outside, or vice versa. It wasn't rocket science to figure out that I wasn't especially safe, not with eight thousand dollars stashed in my luggage. That was a lifetime income for many here. I would have to find an alternative.

I took a taxi across town to the Kazakhstan Hotel. I checked in after observing that it had a single controlled entrance. As it turned out, my concern for security was not misplaced. Two French journalists were beaten up and robbed on the street just outside the Kazakhstan Hotel my first night in Almaty.

Though a bit more secure, my new hotel was still very Soviet. The bed consisted of planks protruding from the wall, a thin mattress, and a board at the end of the planks, high enough to keep your feet from sticking out. If you were tall at all you had to sleep curled in a semifetal position. This type of bed was standard in hotels everywhere in the NIS.

The Soviet system of "one-temperature-for-all" was still in effect, meaning heat came to buildings from a central location. Before the full onslaught of winter, but during weeks when the temperatures were very, very cold, even hotels had no heat.

Prior to leaving for Almaty, I had been advised that I would need to pay for any meetings with government officials. A crisp one hundred dollar bill tucked in an envelope was the fee *du jour*. When I spoke with Sergey about this custom, he offered a fresh perspective on the practice that I had not viewed in quite that way before. To the Russian way of thinking, nothing was free, including business information. Why shouldn't they charge for it? They are acting as consultants, providing information that might be essential to success. Given the dreadfully low wages of these government officials in Russia, Kazakhstan, even India or Egypt, why shouldn't they be properly compensated?

Put this way, I realized this is essentially the foundation of accommodation the world over, indeed the Holy Grail of accommodation. The practice is simply a way to manipulate outcome using money, power, or privilege.

In the mud, the disparity between "haves" and "have nots," with the "have nots" often holding immense bureaucratic power, is the fundamental basis for the system. Accommodation is certainly not limited to lesser-developed environments, it's just easier to recognize. No, accommodation exists everywhere, and it can be quite sophisticated and transparent.

Cultural Snapshot

I went to the hotel restaurant one evening, sat down, and asked for a menu. A weary waiter said in decent English that I would be served what they had. That turned out to be something looking like beef stroganoff, although I use the words loosely. After nibbling a little of the strange concoction, I balked at eating more. Instead, I settled on drinking a couple of imported German beers that I was able to convince the waiter, another term I use very loosely, to bring me.

I requested the bill, and after about twenty minutes, it was brought to my table. I converted the *tenge* into dollars and thought I was suffering the effects of jet lag. I converted again and came up with the same result. *This is impossible*, I thought, *or else there has been a mistake*. My bill totaled about $1.25.

In addition to the food, the value of which I had to admit must be nil, the two German beers absolutely cost the hotel more than my entire bill. The absence of business understanding was not just endemic, it was cultural.

A Turkish Dilemma:
A Lesson in Risk Assessment

Due to the heavy passenger traffic to Germany, I had been forced to book my return flight from Kazakhstan on Turkish Airlines through Istanbul. Waiting for my flight, which was four hours late, I met an American who worked with the U.S. Embassy. I sat next to him in the boarding area where, during idle conversation, he casually mentioned the cholera epidemic in Almaty.

That bit of news exploded in my inattentive brain like a bomb. I'd heard nothing about cholera and seen no signs anywhere. Cholera is taken very seriously everywhere in the world and is often dealt with by quarantine. Now quite alert, I asked what he knew.

"Oh, it's probably nothing," he said, "but the Turks take these rumors very seriously indeed." He explained that when we landed in Turkey, those people not having a health certificate from the U.S. Embassy in Almaty would have to go into quarantine. This was not good. I had no health certificate, but I wasn't about to go into quarantine in Turkey.

The flight departed Almaty and made a scheduled stopover in Tashkent, Uzbekistan. A few passengers got off, others boarded, and soon we took off for Istanbul. After takeoff, the pilot announced the ominous news several times. I was completely preoccupied with thinking of a way to avoid being quarantined. What could I do without a health certificate?

I went through my things hoping to find inspiration and, in the process, studied my ticket. This day I was carrying some good luck. The inbound, nonstop flight from Istanbul to Almaty had one flight number, and the flight out for the stopover in Tashkent, had the *same* number. When I had checked in at the Almaty airport, I was actually taking two flights: the last leg of Flight 100 to Tashkent from Istanbul and Flight 200 from Tashkent to Istanbul. Never mind that I was still on the same plane. Odd and confusing, I realize, but on this day it was serendipitous.

When I'd checked in, the ticketing representative had given me two boarding passes, one marked *Almaty*, the other *Tashkent*. The idea gelled about halfway to Istanbul that I might use the Tashkent pass to avoid quarantine. I realized I was going to have to commit to a course of action after the plane landed and be prepared to ignore the consequences. I knew I couldn't be afraid of making a bad decision because I really didn't know which situation was worse. I wasn't completely sure if I would get in trouble if caught, and I wasn't completely sure what was in store in the "cholera clinic."

As we approached Istanbul, the flight attendants explained the procedure the passengers were to follow when we arrived. There would be two lines. The folks from Almaty had to go to the left, and everyone else, to the right.

After the plane landed, six doctors in white coats wearing grim expressions were waiting for us. Those who had boarded in Tashkent were directed toward stairs leading up to the arrivals hall. The Almaty passengers were purposefully motioned away from the terminal. *I'm going for it*, I thought. I saw in my mind the detention room from the movie *Midnight Express*. That wasn't going to happen to me. *They're going to have to tackle me to get me into quarantine.* I held out my Tashkent boarding pass and put it on top of my American passport.

Outside, practically everyone was filing left. I jumped into the line going to the right, up the stairs. A uniformed guard and a civilian wearing a hospital laboratory jacket were carefully checking Tashkent boarding passes or health certificates from the few Almaty passengers who had them. I was worried they might also have a list of passengers and be checking names against a boarding manifest. I handed the guard my pass. He read out loud "Tashkent," and handed it back to me. He did not check it against another list. Off I went like a shot, flying up the steps to the lobby to lose myself in the arrivals crowd as quickly as I could.

Exhilarated by my escape, I realized this was in microcosm a wonderful example of how risk assessment affected problem solving. Risk assessment is inherent in any problem-solving process and is essential to choosing a path of decision.

In this instance, the available information didn't favor the outcome of either decision. The only thing I did know was that the downside of taking no risk, basically going with the Almaty passengers, was poor. On the other hand, defying the quarantine order could have been more problematic. The risk assessment, as is so often the case, was a toss up.

Unless risk was slam-dunk clear, I usually found it important to be very careful of overanalyzing it. The lesson here is not to get what I call analysis paralysis. Pick a path, commit, and move.

Urals Bandits:
A Lesson in Mafia Law

In late 1993, Sergey and I headed off for a series of client meetings in Moscow. The Merck shipment I had set up in August had been successfully delivered two weeks earlier. While enjoying a wonderful dinner at the restaurant of the newly built Aerostar Hotel, I was told a fascinating story that offered a revealing look at the prevalence of organized crime in the new republics, and an insightful explanation of it.

Joining us at this magnificent dinner of steak and caviar was Gennady, Sergey's cousin by marriage. Gennady had accompanied the Merck shipment on its journey from Moscow to Almaty. He spoke almost no English, so Sergey translated his vivid account of the escapade. Gennady, I understood, was first and foremost a survivor. I later learned he was also the quintessential operator.

Gennady, not tall, bald, and having a penchant for wearing brightly hued clothing, had been a cab driver in the Soviet days, a difficult job to obtain because it meant possible contaminating contact with foreigners and their hard currency. The first qualification to be a taxi driver was to own a car, which was almost impossible in the Soviet era for ordinary citizens without connections. Gennady had also been a car salesman, another difficult and prized job to come by, which was probably how he had acquired his own car.

Gennady, I also learned, had spent a few months in a Soviet jail for illegal currency exchanges. He was one of those guys who had stared Communism down every day. God love him. Sergey had once again found the perfect character for the job.

Gennady was a great natural storyteller. I could see that, even if I didn't understand a word he was saying. Sergey delivered a running commentary, but Gennady was so animated that, after a while, it was almost like hearing it without a translation. What an adventure Gennady's trip to Almaty had been.

Gennady and the driver of the trailer had to reach Almaty by early November, before the Russian winter set in. The entire route was on narrow two-lane, 1930s-style roads in the usual deplorable, Soviet condition.

Inside the trailer rode two armed escorts hired to accompany and to ensure the arrival of the shipment to Almaty. These guards were outfitted in full SWAT gear—camouflage-streaked uniforms, flak jackets, helmets, face guards. Each carried a machine gun and, as former soldiers, they knew how to handle themselves in bad situations.

The Merck ride was relatively uneventful until the truck reached the Ural Mountains and approached the border of Kazakhstan. On a long flat stretch of road, through bleak, deserted country, two cars began to follow the truck trailer. The hired driver saw the cars pull closer to the truck through his side mirrors and shrugged to Gennady, almost as if to say, "They're here." One car passed the truck and pulled ahead of it. Then the car in front began to brake, forcing the truck to slow down. The second car pulled alongside. One of the men motioned for the truck driver to pull over.

The driver did so immediately. As the vehicles stopped, four men stepped out of each car, all eight of them heavily armed. Gennady and the driver climbed down from the truck. One of the eight greeted them cordially. "Hello, how are you?" said their leader. "My name is Mikhail. We're sure that you didn't know this, but we own this section of the road. We find your trailer using it without our permission. There is a penalty for that in these parts. We're going to take your trailer."

Gennady remained silent as he waited for the unfolding events. The truck driver, who frequently used the route, was obviously very familiar with the whole routine. He said, "You know, of course, the trailer isn't mine."

Mikhail shrugged. "We understand, and we're very sorry about that. In any event, you must give it to us."

The driver continued calmly, "The people who are to receive the trailer have hired someone whom you must speak with, and they are inside."

"Very well," said the leader. At that point, the doors opened at the rear of the container and out stepped the two armed guards, weapons ready. There were two sharp clicks as safeties went off the triggers of the machine guns. "That was a scene right out of a movie," Gennady said with a smile. "It was like Rambo and the Terminator both stepping out of that trailer."

"We have been hired by the owners of this trailer to escort it to Almaty," one of the armed guards said. "That is our mission."

Gennady had thought there would be mayhem and destruction. But no, a different etiquette prevailed. Mikhail said, "We understand. We didn't know. We apologize. But you do know that the owner made a mistake."

The other soldier said, "We didn't know about a mistake." Gennady stressed the word "know" passed back and forth with several inflections.

The driver then spoke up. "We all agree now that a mistake has been made by the owner of the truck. How can we compensate you for your trouble?"

The armed men graciously accepted two hundred dollars in American cash on the spot, and the incident ended. After pocketing the money, Mikhail said, "We will escort you the rest of the way to the border of Kazakhstan. Hard as it is to believe, there are thieves here. We will be your *krisha*."

With a pleasant good-bye, they returned to their cars. Gennady said, "The two armed soldiers climbed back into the trailer and we were rolling again in five minutes. The cars stayed with us for the next fifty miles then remained until we reached the border. There, the men waved us across into Kazakhstan." He took another bite of caviar and said, "The whole incident was very cordial."

The story wasn't finished. Some miles across the border, well into Kazakhstan, another car stopped the truck. This time, there were only four armed bandits from one vehicle, who seemed almost bored as they went through the motions. Gennady didn't even get out of the truck. The words were the same: "This is our territory. Since you did not get our permission, we must take your trailer." "I understand," said the driver. "We regret a mistake was made. Would you discuss this with the owner's representatives in the trailer?"

"We will speak with them. Oh… yes. We see how it is."

"How can we compensate you for our mistake?" Another two hundred dollars and the bandits left.

The story was truly amazing. Through Sergey, I inquired of Gennady whether the driver had indicated if this was normal or if cargo was ever lost. Once Gennady got the translation of my question he animatedly explained that the driver had informed him that *most* of the time the cargo was taken. Gennady explained that had the armed SWAT guards not been present, the Merck shipment would have been a goner.

I was fascinated by the cordiality of the confrontation and remarked as such. Sergey said this was normal. Mafia types nearly always made their initial requests in polite terms. Even the second requests were made politely, though more forcefully. Then Sergey lowered his voice and ominously declared that it was at the third request that no one was left alive to remember how pleasantly it had all started.

I also asked Sergey what the first bandits had meant by *krisha*. Sergey looked me square in the eye and replied, "Ron, everything in Russia concerns having a roof." *Krisha* means "roof" in Russian

In typically Russian parable style, Sergey went on to say that, of course, everyone must have a roof over his head. I understood the allegorical terminology perfectly— without a roof, all sorts of bad weather could befall a person. I had just received my first very valuable understanding of the Russian concept of *krisha* and how it applied to the Mafia in particular.

As I had in Nigeria and Thailand, I was coming to understand the law, or really lack thereof, in Russia. A generalization of my legal insights was developing, a realization that all environments develop some type of informal system, or "law of the land."

This story and all its ramifications became critically important to my actions in the near future.

Sign of the Times

I was coming to see that post-Soviet Russia, in reality, was not so different from the multilayered entity depicted in John Le Carre's novels. There was the Mafia, rarely seen, but hovering just out of sight. As a counterbalance to the Mafia, the private sector had many former intelligence officers and security guards—ex-special forces—who could be brutally and often fatally competent when provoked. The fall of the Soviet Union was a commercial windfall for all the CIA, NSA, KGB, and other spooks looking to get into private business. They were everywhere.

It was also like something out of the roaring '20s in the United States. Everyone, it seemed, was out on the night having a very good time indeed. Anything went. Every Western businessman walking the streets in the daytime carried cash, with much more stashed in his hotel room. That was commercial life in Russia—on the edge, raw, unnerving at times, but fed everywhere by a driving sense that millions could be made in the new economy.

Whenever I went, I was immediately surrounded by Russians asking the new refrain, "Are you looking to do business?"

An Address in Vienna:
A Lesson in Effective Translation

Having surmounted so many difficulties and realized a fair measure of success, I had never felt more able. Everything that came about in my endeavors in Russia followed familiar patterns of the work I had done, and past lessons kept resurfacing. Business just exploded.

In early 1994 I was asked to be a speaker at a major conference in Vienna, Austria. The conference was on the status of logistics infrastructure (e.g., roads, bridges, customs, etc.) in the former Soviet Union and was sponsored by the Adam Smith Institute of London. A representative of the Institute contacted me requesting my participation as a featured speaker, and I accepted the invitation, as I felt it was very likely the conference would be attended by dozens of potential clients seeking advice on the perils of shipping goods and equipment into the new republics.

I had been assigned the topic of outlining the problems inherent in shipping into this newly accessible region of the world. In deciding how to best present the problems in a fitting perspective, I arrived at the idea of letting the headlines of newspapers around the world define the problems. I prepared transparencies of relevant headlines screaming from newspapers across Europe and the United States. They described obstacles such as fuel shortages, customs delays, and the cross border disputes in the war-torn areas of Tajikistan, Armenia, and Chechnya. All this, plus the ever-present problems of theft, and even murder, at the hands of organized crime, was part of the presentation.

In preparation for the speech, I also asked Sergey to give me a tutorial on how to make an introduction in Russian. Sergey coached me on the correct pronunciation and format of an approximately thirty-word Russian introduction.

I arrived in Vienna from St. Petersburg the night before the conference began and checked into the Intercontinental Hotel. I was scheduled to speak on the afternoon of first day of the two-day gathering.

Entering the hall that morning, I really had no idea of what to expect. I was surprised at the number of attendees, somewhere between four and five hundred. The smallest portion of those assembled were Americans, with the majority hailing from Europe and a good third from the New Republics. The dais was raised some five feet and extended about forty feet across the large hall, giving even those even in the rear a good view of the speakers.

On each side of the hall were two enclosed translation booths, one for English to Russian and the other for Russian to English. The state-of-the-art booths broadcast translations simultaneously for each speaker. Upon entering, each conference participant was handed a tiny set of earphones attached to a small battery-powered antennae receiver that could be put in a jacket pocket or attached to a dress.

The size of the gathering and the big-league atmosphere definitely increased the nervousness I was feeling. I was especially apprehensive about properly delivering the Russian introduction Sergey had coached me through. I fretted the entire morning about whether or not I should scrap it.

My time to speak arrived, and I stayed with the Russian introduction, confusing the interpreter. That should have been a warning sign to me. The Russian introduction went over well with the crowd, however, and I was given a patter of applause for the attempt. With the tough part successfully behind me, I plunged into the main gist of the presentation. One by one, I placed the twenty or so transparencies onto the projector, displaying them onto a one hundred square foot screen, and covered the various topics.

I was very relieved when I finished. The presentation had been a lot of work to prepare, and I had been worried that it was dull. The absolute worst thing you can do as a speaker is to be boring. The comments I received from the Americans and Europeans in the crowd suggested that the presentation had been well received as both informative and interesting. The comments from the New Republic attendees, however, were a completely different matter.

I was stunned to learn the speech had not been well received by many of the Russian and other New Republic ministers. I was approached by one of the Russian ministers on hand and informed, through an interpreter, that he and others had been insulted by my speech. Now, as a precaution against just this kind of occurrence, I had gone over the presentation with Sergey. He had assured me that my remarks would not anger or offend.

Inquiring what exactly had offended the minister, I discovered the English to Russian interpreter had given my presentation a meaning that had not been intended. My words had been delivered in an accusatory tone, as if I were saying to those from the New Republics that all the problems were *their* fault. *That* tone, or message, had not been intended. Unaware of this tone, I had been unable to correct the interpreter's slant on my words. How could I have been? I don't speak Russian.

It was my most troubling and revealing lesson yet on the pitfalls of communicating via interpreters. The interpreter had correctly communicated the words, but had added her editorial tone. It was a communications lesson in misinterpretation in the truest sense.

What should I have done differently? I should have had my own interpreter there to make sure the interpretation I expected was indeed relayed. When situations are important and the outcome critical, having a check on translation is essential.

A Soviet Legacy:
A Lesson in Bargaining

On a trip to Moscow, I had dinner with a steamship line representative I first met in Amsterdam the previous year. Howard, a thirtyish, stoutly built American, had been transferred to Russia not long after our first meeting. The dinner in Moscow with Howard was remarkable for a perplexing story on negotiation.

It was a very cold evening in Moscow, about ten degrees below Celsius or fourteen degrees Fahrenheit, and snowing to beat the band. Howard came into the restaurant wearing one of those very Russian fur hats, looking for all the world, just like a "Russkie" to my eye. I remarked on how warm the hat looked and on the near perfect fit. Finding anything in Russia in those days that was anywhere close to perfect immediately demanded scrutiny. Howard explained how he had come by the hat.

In those days, Russian stores usually contained a hodgepodge of items. There was no such thing as a hat store—if you were out and saw a hat, or two, you bought them. Howard's wife and three children had joined him in Russia, so he needed hats for all of them and, of course, for himself. For just such a happenstance, Howard had been carrying four different length strings, each measuring the respective circumferences of his wife and children's heads to ensure he bought the correct sizes. Items couldn't be returned—the concept was little known—so whatever he bought was his forever. The remarkable negotiation story comes from the encounter Howard had in a store where he spotted three fur hats.

Inspecting the fur hats, all three matched his string measuring guides. Howard decided that, since he needed two more hats, he would inquire if the store owner could have them made. The owner spoke decent English and said that, indeed, she could make two more fur hats. Howard had struck a proverbial gold mine of hats. The three fur hats were priced at approximately twenty-five dollars each, so Howard decided, naturally, to bargain for the five. This made perfect sense to him. He reasoned that if he bought five hats he should get a discount, a perfectly reasonable assumption in most parts of the world, but not here.

Howard asked the owner to make the two other hats and offered her one hundred and ten dollars, a small discount of fifteen dollars, for all five. The lady furrowed her brow, obviously intensely debating the offer, or so Howard thought. No, she declared, she would have to be paid one hundred and fifty dollars for five. Her price included a premium of twenty-five dollars.

Howard was sure the woman had misunderstood him, so he explained more slowly and even did the math on a piece of paper for her to see. The lady waited patiently through his explanation. When he finished, she stated that she understood perfectly, it was *he* who didn't understand. The two additional hats would have to be *made* thus requiring *more work*. That was why there was a premium. She went on to say that if he argued any further, she wouldn't make them at all.

Howard was dumbfounded. Every economic principle he had ever been taught was violated in that negotiation. Instantly realizing he was in danger of losing his two additional hats and that it could be weeks before he found others, he agreed to the woman's asking price for all five hats.

Howard's perception of his leverage was incorrect. Never mind it was the right perception in just about every other place in the world. By pressing the negotiation with incorrectly perceived leverage, he essentially worsened his position. In a distorted way, due to the local predilection for avoiding work, the Russian lady held the leverage.

Never before, or since, have I come across a more enlightening account of the importance of understanding the *perception* of leverage in a negotiation.

After our enjoyable dinner that cold, snowy evening, I did not see Howard again in Russia. A chilling story circulated concerning the circumstances of his departure. The steamship line he worked for was importing expensive automobiles, Mercedes and the like, from Europe bound for dealerships in the NIS. A legend grew that Howard was approached, very courteously, one day by two men. They nicely requested that he turn over to them one automobile from each vessel that arrived at the port. Howard replied that he couldn't comply with their request and hurriedly departed their company.

The next ship arrived and unloaded its cargo of expensive autos. The very next day Howard received another visit from the same two men, again demanding an auto from each vessel. Howard left Russia that night, never to return.

A Conversation with Lenin:
A Lesson in Cultural Hypocrisy

On my first trip to Moscow in 1992, I took the short walk from the Metropol Hotel, around the Lenin Museum, to the massive plaza that is Red Square. Flanked on one side by the Kremlin Walls and on another by St. Basil's Cathedral, it's an impressive sight. I recall being very uncomfortable by the stares I drew from the locals, who could tell from the make of my clothing that I was not Russian. The main point of interest then was the fact that Lenin's Tomb, where he lay preserved, embalmed and partially reconstructed of wax, was closed. Rumor had it that he was to be removed, as if carting off his remains might wipe away the blight in which he had enveloped this huge country for nearly seventy years.

Two years later, I was again in Moscow and met up with friends from the States who were in Russia to adopt a baby. I, Sergey, and another associate from my office in Alexandria gave them a tour of the city on May Day. It was still an official holiday but minus the Soviet-era huge parade of weapons filing through Red Square. Our group first went to lunch, following the Russian custom of imbibing a bit, then we went to Red Square in the afternoon. Lo and behold, Lenin's Tomb was open. We decided to take a look.

Entering the tomb, I was totally unprepared for the extreme and artificial reverence being enforced. Russian military guards where shushing people and threatening to remove and arrest anyone talking as they proceeded through. To ensure utmost quiet we were even required to put cloth covers over our shoes. It was all too much. As we entered the eerily lit chamber and passed along a raised railed walkway, *there he was*, only a few feet away in a glass-covered open casket.

During the time I'd been coming to the former Soviet Union, I'd witnessed firsthand the legacy of Communism—abject poverty, crumbled buildings, and rampant alcoholism. Nothing worked properly. Lenin was the perpetrator of all the unhappiness and devastation, and he was being treated like Jesus or something. This went through my mildly inebriated brain as I gazed upon the yellowed head.

I'm not sure what came over me, maybe it was a combination of the beers at lunch and the overdone reverence, but I was compelled to give Lenin a piece of my mind. As I reached the center of the tomb, only four feet or so from his embalmed skull, I leaned over the railing and said, just loudly enough so that were he alive he could have easily heard me, "Pssst, Vlad baby, you were *wrong!*"

I was half wishing for a voice to come back to me from the corpse saying, "I know," or at least a suppressed chuckle followed by, "Well, it worked for a while, didn't it?"

Those next to me, who were equally tipsy, heard my admonition to Vladimir and started snickering. Very quickly it became uncontrollable. We tried, somewhat unsuccessfully, to stifle irrepressible laughter. Hurrying toward the exit, we were met by guards looking and acting as if they would shoot us for our sacrilege. Out the tomb door we flew, where we exploded with laughter. The guards menacingly threatened to detain us unless we departed immediately.

The aftermath of the affront to Lenin left us all with the realization of the undeniable cultural confusion that the Russian people carry regarding the memory of Lenin. Even though the past had been dreadful, due almost completely to his ideals, there existed a strong desire to hold on to the ideals he represented. This misguided, culturally based allegiance to, and pursuit of, ideals is not so uncommon. I would encounter a surprising correlation to this in corporate culture before long.

Almaty Mystery:
A Lesson in Examining the Source

I had hired a former CIA man, Barry, who headed up our new office in Almaty. He didn't do a bad job, but his own interests inevitably led to problems.

After five months in Almaty, Barry called and told me that we had major Mafia problems. He insisted we had to close the office and informed me that he was quitting. I immediately called Sergey to seek his opinion. Sergey was of the opinion that any Mafia problems in Almaty might be personal to Barry, arising from his CIA days. I called Barry back and explained that I didn't want to close the office. I would be sending down a temporary replacement, Mike, followed shortly by one of my managers, John. Barry agreed to remain in place until they arrived and a transition took place.

Before he left, I went over the situation with Mike. I explained that, should he be worried at all about his safety while in Almaty, he was free to leave immediately for Moscow or Europe. Although Barry continued his ominous warnings, the two weeks prior to John's arrival in Almaty were uneventful. When John arrived, the unnerving warnings increased. Barry kept insinuating that it was the company that had a problem with the local Mafia, that everyone should leave, and that the office should be closed.

A few days passed without problems, and the worrisome situation seemed to abate. Then, a nasty shock came as Barry, John, and Mike left the office for dinner one night. Driving everyone in his car, Barry kept glancing anxiously in the rearview mirror en route to the restaurant. He even made a few U-turns in the streets, giving the impression they were being followed.

Barry's antics made both my guys very nervous, and dinner became an afterthought. When the three of them walked out of the restaurant after their meal, two oversized men accosted Barry. "Come over and talk to us," they told him in English. John and Mike remained together by the restaurant door while the goons hustled Barry some forty feet away—speaking in Russian and not in conversational tones. It was clear these were not friends.

Barry, wide-eyed, walked back to Mike and John. "We all have to leave right now," he said with obvious fear. "Just pack, go to the airport, and take the first plane out." Mike and John were now scared out of their wits. After rushing back to their hotel, Mike and John phoned me at home explaining the events of the evening. I immediately called Sergey to get his thoughts.

Again, Sergey said he thought the matter, whatever it was, between Barry and his antagonists had been personal. He didn't believe it pertained to our business. Sergey's advise was to move the office immediately as he felt this would help to separate any perceived connection to Barry.

Barry took his own advice and left Almaty that next morning on a flight to Europe. Meanwhile, Mike and John rented a new office across town and moved all of the files and equipment. One day, then two, turned into a week with no further contact.

I realize the mere relocation of the office seems trivial, but I saw logic in play that was wrapped up in local beliefs. I understood a bit about the basis of Sergey's reasoning, but I would not have reached the same conclusion. The insight began to form that while local or foreign logic can often lead to disastrous incidents like those perpetrated by the Masai guide and the Nigerian taxi driver, it can also be brilliant.

For the next few suspenseful weeks, we all waited to see if the Mafia would make contact again. The "problem" in Almaty still lingered, and I knew I had to put the situation to rest. I had to go to Almaty and soon. I was going to the source. The path I chose was reliant upon Sergey's logic regarding the Mafia issue and my own understanding of the law of the land. I hoped I was correct on all assumptions.

I met Sergey in Moscow as planned, and we boarded the Transaero aircraft for the four-hour flight. We had been in the air for about an hour and were having cocktails when delayed reality set in. All the other risky situations I had faced over the years came rushing through my mind, and they all seemed to pale in comparison to the potential confrontation looming. My adrenaline was pumping something fierce. Toward the end of our first cocktail, I said to Sergey, "Okay, we land. Let's say we have a contact. What then?"

Sergey looked at me, and then very calmly reached into his pocket and extracted a slip of paper with a telephone number written on it. "Ron," he said, "if we have contact with the Mafia, we call this number, and we'll have no problem." It was a local number in Almaty, not a Moscow number.

I didn't ask him how he had come by that number. Obviously Sergey had done some thorough research before leaving Moscow, and I left it at that. I assumed that he had gone to a *krisha* and told him our potential problem.

The itinerary I had planned put Sergey and me in Almaty for two days before leaving for two days in Kyrgyzstan. Then, we were back in Almaty for two days before departing. Plenty of time for a contact, if one was to be made. Sergey and I were sitting on eggshells for almost a week.

The first two days passed as if they were two months. Thankfully, they were uneventful. On the third morning, we departed by car for the half-day journey into Kyrgyzstan and it's capital, Bishkek.

Our hotel in Bishkek, if you could call it that, was nothing more than a cluster of cinderblocks piled one on top of another. The rooms had corroded toilets and ice-cold running water—so cold it turned my fingers blue—and no heat at night. During the day you could be quite warm in the sun, but at night, it was wickedly cold. With the temperature near zero, I slept each night in every piece of clothing I had with me, every shirt and T-shirt, socks and shoes, including my jacket. There were two blankets on the bed. One I kept around my feet—the other I wrapped around my neck and head. To add to the misery, the cold did not stop a parade of oversized, very healthy cockroaches. In the mornings, the water was so cold I couldn't get my shaving cream to lather, and a shower was out of the question. Those two days, while uneventful, passed like years.

Returning to Almaty, the remaining two days of our journey also went very slowly. Although we never spoke about it, Sergey and I were exceedingly apprehensive. You could cut the tension with a knife. If there was to be a contact, it would be then. Finally, the morning of our departure arrived. As we boarded the plane for Moscow, I turned to him and said, "No contact."

Sergey replied. "I've been thinking about that every moment."

Indeed, it appeared the issue had been personal to Barry and the logic correct, and so had been the understanding of the law of the land. Without the crutch of my lessons, I don't think I could have gone down that path. And, just as on the trip to Zimbabwe, the problem was solved by going to the source.

White House Echoes:
A Lesson in Saving Political Face

As a result of the end of the cold war and the warming of relations between the United States and the New Republics, the republics of Russia, Ukraine, Kazakhstan, and Belarus entered into an agreement with the United States named the Cooperative Threat Reduction (CTR) Treaty. This treaty's purpose was to begin dismantling many of their nuclear weapons. In practice, this meant that the United States would provide the necessary money, and, in most cases, the means to the all-but-bankrupt post-Soviet governments in order to begin disarmament.

Hughes Technical Systems Corporation, the government services division of the Hughes Aircraft Company in the United States, had decided to bid on one of the early CTR contracts to establish maintenance and logistics service bases that were also to be a part of the weapons destruction verification system. Hughes asked my company to participate as a subcontractor on their bid.

The forthcoming contract shortly immersed me in circumstances that echoed all the way to the White House. Thus also began, from a genesis standpoint, a series of events that resulted in the sale of my company.

In early November, I was back in Moscow specifically to address a situation that was threatening to be nothing short of an international dilemma. The Communists had not been out of power all that long in the New Republics. It was no surprise that, even though Yeltsin and the other respective political leaders had entered into the CTR agreement for disarmament, those actually charged with implementation were suspicious of the whole arrangement. An ongoing dispute over the protocols involved in the agreement rocked the new Russian Republic.

A major stumbling block to the implementation of the agreement was that Russia wanted the necessary CTR dismantlement equipment delivered into Russian hands at their borders. The official U.S. position was that all equipment and spare parts delivered for the dismantlement of Russian nuclear and conventional weapons had to be in U.S. government control until final delivery to the highly guarded military bases and secret cities. The Russians were saying *nyet, no.*

For months, the Russians steadfastly denied the U.S. government and its contractors the ability to move any CTR equipment past Russian borders. Essentially, the Cooperative Threat Reduction Treaty, a national security level treaty, was in danger of collapsing if the Russians would not relent. The highest levels of the U.S. government—which we were told included the White House—were following this dilemma closely.

The issue remained unresolved and came to affect the contract we had with Hughes. That cold November day, I was in Moscow for a high-level meeting among the U.S. government, the contractors, and the heads of the Russian Ministry overseeing the implementation of the treaty.

The contractors' contingent had gathered at the entrance of the Moscow Slavenskaya Hotel when Bob, the Hughes manager, approached and informed me that the Russians were pulling their usual shenanigans. Shumkov, a high-ranking minister of the Committee for Defense Industries (CDI), part of the Russian Defense Ministry, wanted fewer people in attendance due to security concerns. That was probably bull, but it was meant to be a clear signal that the Russians were in charge. As a result, I decided to have Sergey represent the company. I felt the meeting would be a complete waste of time. Man, was I wrong.

Shortly after two o'clock that afternoon, Sergey came back from the meeting and gave me the details. In fairly typical Russian fashion, Shumkov had blustered and lectured the Americans. No dialogue took place, just a hardening of the Russian position.

Sergey told me that as an appeal to Shumkov, the American delegation explained that the United States had contracted with a Russian Joint Venture, employing Russians, to move the equipment to the secret cities and military bases. Shumkov immediately seized on this. "What do you mean?" he said belligerently. The U.S. delegation explained that the U.S. contractors had a Russian company, represented by Sergey. Shumkov glared at Sergey, "Who are you? Why are you here?"

Sergey responded just as adamantly, "I am a Russian businessman. I have established one of the first joint operations with the Americans. I am part of the new economy in Russia."

Amazingly, Sergey's response altered Shumkov's entire demeanor. He began asking him questions about his business in an entirely different, even cordial, manner. The meeting had changed directions, and everyone there knew it.

"So," Shumkov said, "*Russians* will be handling this equipment and the spare parts once they cross our borders." Sergey nodded. Shumkov continued, "Russians in your Russian company, not Americans." Again Sergey nodded.

"You see," Shumkov said turning to the Americans, "*now* we are solving this problem, yes?"

News that Shumkov had retreated from the intransigent Russian position and that a way had been found out of the disagreement spread quickly all the way to the White House, or so we were told. The log jam had been broken— the multi-billion dollar nuclear arms reduction program could go forward.

Despite the effects of a lingering Communist paranoia, the real concept of maintaining face was at work here. Shumkov had, in retrospect, been looking for way out of the impasse. He had found it by attaching great significance that Russians should handle the necessary tasks within Russian borders, albeit Russians working in joint venture with Americans. The fact that he had genuinely liked Sergey and found a face-saving compromise was one of those fortuitous events that, in instances just as this, can have amazing ramifications. In this case, my little company had directly impacted the Russian-U.S. political relationship in a big way.

What I learned from the Shumkov incident and others to follow was that whenever an endeavor is important, when stakes are at their highest, maintaining face supersedes logical behavior.

It would not be the last time my company and I were in the middle of a high-stakes poker game between the United States and another government.

A Hex, a Babushka, and an Introduction: A Lesson in Communicating with the Locals

Daily life in Russia and the New Republics was anything but routine. That went triple for traveling in the NIS. There were so many instances when I thought I was on *Candid Camera* that I sometimes found myself looking around for the hidden lens. Never mind the outlandishness of what was *taking place*, I often had to pinch myself to make sure I wasn't dreaming. Such was the case in the following three stories.

Sergey and I headed to Kiev, Ukraine in early summer of 1995. It was a morning flight and, as had become our custom, we stopped at the Novotel Hotel near the Sheremetyevo airport terminals for breakfast. We figured that we might not have time for lunch that day since immediately following the three hour flight to Kiev we would board a specially chartered aircraft to take us to the Ukrainian port city of Mariopol.

The Novotel had a great breakfast buffet, but the real reason we went there was that it served the best coffee in Moscow. Being a coffee lover, it was my sad experience that it was usually impossible to find a decent cup in the "mud." When I did, as had been the case in Mogadishu, I was like a junkie in search of a fix. Joined by Gennady, Sergey and I leisurely ate breakfast before jumping back into his Lada for the two minute drive over to Sheremetyevo I.

Sergey and I walked to the end of the terminal where the Kiev flights *usually* departed. We arrived at the regular gate, marked by a big sign that said "Kiev" in Cyrillic, and joined the line. Upon reaching the front, we were told that this plane was not going to Kiev. Sergey asked where the Kiev flight was, and the lady just shrugged.

We had very little time. Sergey and I raced down the terminal with our bags in tow. Sergey asked each gate agent if that plane was going to Kiev— none of the signs over the gates showed the correct destination. We found our gate with only minutes to spare. Fortunately, the last of the passengers had just passed the boarding gate agent.

We handed our tickets to the very bureaucratic female ticketing agent standing at the counter only to have her announce very authoritatively in Russian to Sergey, "Check in is over." He relayed this to me, and I was dumbfounded. The end of the boarding line of passengers was only ten feet from where Sergey and I stood. It was so typical. The gates were all marked wrong; the line was mere feet away, and we're screwed. I *must* be in Russia.

To make matters as bad as possible, no other flights to Kiev were scheduled for the next two days. We had to take *this* plane. The chartered flight in Kiev would cost thousands to delay, and my schedule to return to the States absolutely prevented me from waiting two days. To further complicate the matter, we were carrying fifty thousand dollars in cash that *had* to be in Mariopol soon. A very large CTR operation depended upon it. I asked Sergey to generally explain our situation to her.

Sergey plead our case to the officious agent. She merely shrugged indifferently. I was getting angry at the absurd scenario. The slow moving line of boarding passengers was still only feet away. Sergey was now dejected. I asked him, not in the least bit expecting what happened next, to say something, *anything* to her that was insulting. No longer expecting to make the plane, I just wanted to be certain the gate agent knew what I thought of her, and I didn't speak enough Russian to do it myself.

Sergey fixed her eye with a look I'd never want to see directed at me. He said very calmly in Russian, "I wish upon you bad luck some day, that you have this same problem, and that you miss something very important in your life."

He delivered it like a curse, and it had an immediate effect. Russians are very superstitious, and this gate agent was no exception. She looked at Sergey, instantly realizing that he had hexed her. Her eyes widened, and her demeanor softened. Without a word, she took our tickets and let us join the line of boarding passengers.

It was incredible. Taking our seats, Sergey explained that he *knew* he had said something that would upset her. Amazingly obvious to me was that *both* Sergey and the overbearing agent absolutely believed the hex would come to fruition had she not let us pass. Most importantly, we got on that flight, and it was due solely to that unusual negotiation.

In this "negotiation," the leverage had been a hex. And, without question, both the ticket agent and Sergey perceived the leverage in the same light. My head was shaking all the way to Mariopol. Try finding that lesson at any business school.

While doing business in the NIS, I found dozens of bureaucratic issues that proved onerous. There were constant regulatory changes that were never announced in advance. Out of the blue, a new rule or procedure dominating some aspect of our commercial life would suddenly appear. These changes always offered a unique insight into local logic.

One day, out of nowhere, the Russian Federation arbitrarily decreed that all inter-republic rail scheduling had to be approved in Moscow. Just like that, rail traffic leaving Russia for other republics was stopped cold. It was absolute chaos. We had customer rail shipments stuck all over the place. We weren't alone. Every transporter in the country was in the same fix.

It took Sergey's crew two long days just to learn where the new rail offices were and what the new procedures for rail scheduling were. Once the new scheduling location was found, there were thousands of scheduling petitions already piled up. Making matters worse, the bureaucrat signing the petitions only did so a few hours each day. It was a mess.

In Alexandria, this was brought to my attention during a meeting late one evening. At first blush, I deducted it was an accommodation situation and called Sergey the next day to authorize whatever payments necessary to get our rail petitions signed. By this time, though, the bureaucrat was besieged, and merely getting an audience was impossible. Our rail cars were going nowhere fast.

I called Sergey the following morning and learned that our rail cars were moving. "Atleechna," I said. *Excellent*. "But how did that happen?" The explanation was a blue ribbon case in point illustrating local logic.

After trying to approach the troublesome and lazy bureaucrat without success, Sergey's people located the woman, a grandmotherly babushka type, responsible for cleaning that section of the newly declared rail scheduling offices. They explained to her that we needed all our petitions, currently in the huge pile awaiting signature, to be put on top for the following morning's signing session. The cleaning lady did just that, and, *voila*, the next day our petitions were signed. From that day forward, we took our rail petitions directly to her. Thus was born the slickest rail signatory process around. It was taking our competitors days and even weeks to move inter-republic rail cars. Ours moved almost immediately. An accommodation was made, of course, but it was the genius of the logic that hit me. It was so Russian and, in that light, so logical.

In a restaurant in Almaty, Kazakhstan another lesson in communications was taken. Like the Arabic MA-tar story in Khartoum, it involved the misuse of a foreign language. If ever I wished a camera from a show like *Punk'd* had been filming, it was during this situation. I laughed so hard I cried.

We were attending an international trade show in Almaty, and we all went out to dinner the first evening to one of the new restaurants in town. It turned out to be a quite good Italian restaurant, and it was crowded. After the four of us sat down, Sergey, Brian, a young American hired due to his

Russian fluency, and I became engaged in the continuing process of enlarging my Russian vocabulary. The fourth of our group was Debbie, a petite blonde with a passing resemblance to Meg Ryan, who had decided she was going to learn some basic Russian. Debbie, the quintessential outgoing, uninhibited salesperson had decided that instead of learning individual words she would learn whole phrases such as: "My name is Debbie." Determined to show off her newly acquired command of Russian, just as our waiter approached the table, she loudly proclaimed with an engaging, friendly smile what she thought was, "My name is Debbie."

Instantly, Sergey, Brian, the waiter, and every other patron sitting within earshot were stunned to silence. The waiter's eyes grew round as saucers, and he was obviously uncomfortable. Brian began to snicker and then to laugh uncontrollably. Debbie, believing she had not been understood, decided to repeat herself, this time even louder. Sergey, a very proper guy, tried futilely to shush her. Debbie would have none of it.

Now everyone in the restaurant was looking at our table. Brian was laughing so uncontrollably he was bent over and almost under the table. I, along with Debbie, had no idea what was going on, but I knew it was related to what she had said. The waiter, his body language communicating his immense discomfort, had all he could take and bolted off to the kitchen. I asked Sergey what was going on. Sergey, now laughing almost as hard as Brian, could not speak. Finally, near tears and between gasps of laughter, Brian whispered to me the translation. Debbie was boldly proclaiming herself "Oral Sex Debbie" to the entire restaurant. Immediately, the look on the waiter's face and the bemused, rapt attention of all the patrons made sense. It was a scene right out of the movie *When Harry met Sally* when Harry and Sally are in the restaurant and Sally fakes an orgasm. Within a nanosecond, I, too, was doubled up in laughter. Debbie continued to repeat her phrase, certain she only had to say it even more loudly to be understood. As she repeated herself again and again, the entire restaurant filled with laughter. Debbie's communications predicament was being understood, and enjoyed, by all. Finally, between bouts of laughter, I was able to explain to Debbie why all the patrons in the restaurant were giggling. Unfazed, Debbie merely decided that Russian was just not for her.

As I've stated, it's practically impossible to know every potential language landmine, but it is imperative that one be sensitive to the fact that these landmines exist. Don't stop trying. Everyone appreciates the effort. Just realize that when peoples' eyes widen, and especially when snickers begin, you may have wandered into a communications no man's land similar to Debbie's.

Cultural Snapshot

In many ways, even as convoluted as Russia and the other former Soviet Union countries proved to be, I found my experiences there refreshing. There were very few Russians with whom I came in contact that I did not like. I found them to be open, though also suspicious, by nature. Given their long, dark history, the wonder to me was that they remained open at all. Even more amazingly, the openness dominated if you were introduced by a friend. As far as operating, or even existing, in post-Soviet Russia, nothing was more important than one's network of friends, culturally bound by the glue of the shared experience of enduring such encompassing oppression. The Soviet state had spies literally everywhere and to be "vouched for" as a person worthy of trust was essential. Hence an introduction of a stranger by a friend instantly transformed the stranger into a friend for life.

The Pieter Principle:
A Lesson in Going Back to Basics

It was impossible not to continually take stock of how far my company had progressed in the two short years of our involvement in Russia. Since making the deal with the janitor for the office space, the staff in St. Petersburg had grown to nearly twenty people. The Almaty office was staffed by eight, and we had a Moscow office with a staff of a dozen. A tight-knit group, all had close ties dating to their shared maritime days. They trusted no one who wasn't a proven friend or a relation by blood or marriage.

In my Alexandria office, the staff had nearly tripled to over sixty employees and revenue and profits had tripled as well. This amazing growth was not even close to finished. Over the next year, our profits again nearly tripled. The increase in revenue and profits was wholly due to our expansion into Russia and the NIS.

A new CTR contract was to be awarded for the transport of all of the cutting, digging, and lifting equipment to be used for destroying the conventional and nuclear weapons in Russia, Ukraine, Kazakhstan, and Belarus.

The weapons dismantlement equipment was a fascinating array with even more fascinating intended uses. There were huge cranes, with enormous lift capacity, to be used to lift nuclear warhead–tipped intercontinental ballistic missiles out of their silos. Then there were the many hundreds of special containers for the emptied propellant mixtures.

For aircraft and submarines, there were special cutting implements. The largest of these was called the baler shear, an enormous guillotine. The baler shear had a feeding ramp that went under the guillotine. Basically, the hull of a submarine or fuselage of a plane was rolled under the giant shear, cutting the weapon into sections.

There were also smaller high-tech cutting implements, such as plasma cutters for cutting bombs. There were heat exchangers, rounded pots looking eerily similar to the original little boy, a piece of equipment that melted the components from all the weapons. The melting separated valuable metals like silver and copper for recovery. It was, quite literally, implementing the Old Testament hope of turning swords into plowshares.

It was a lucrative contract, to be sure, and every major transportation company in the United States and Europe with any type of organization or affiliation in the NIS wanted it. It was one of the largest logistics contracts in the world at that point in time, and sixty-five companies requested copies of the bid. In the end, my company won the CTR dismantlement contract.

For all that was going on, it was this CTR contract that required the most attention. From the moment we won the contract, we entered a world that, to that point in time, had only existed for characters in cold war novels. From the briefings we received at the Pentagon warning us about nuclear radiation around Russian submarine bases, to the so-called anthrax town south of Ekaterinburg, to our access to the ultra-secret cities where the Soviets had built their nuclear arsenal, we were in rarified territory.

It should come as no surprise that none of this was easy or simple. It seemed as if every other week, one or another of the weapons dismantlement shipments we were delivering threatened to become an international incident, headlining the front pages of newspapers. Incidents in every new republic often left me wondering what would happen next.

One incident in which I was directly involved seemed destined to become an international incident. "The Standoff", as it came to be known, began with the delivery of two hundred tank cars to an intercontinental missile base called Turinskaya, located in a remote corner of Russia south of eastern Siberia and just north of Mongolia. The distance from St. Petersburg was twenty-five hundred miles, or roughly the distance from New York to Los Angeles. It was about as close to the middle of nowhere as you can get.

The tank cars were intended to hold the rocket fuel to be drained from the aging Russian intercontinental ballistic missiles (ICBM). There were two types of cars, distinguished by different colored stripes painted horizontally across the stainless steel containers. This was because the Soviet missiles used two highly volatile liquids, one the propellant and the other an oxidizer that ignited when mixed together, thus launching the missile.

Pieter, Sergey's brother-in-law and a former colonel in Soviet Army Intelligence, headed what we named our mobile delivery teams. Pieter's teams had to promptly offload the equipment from the rail cars. If we dawdled, there could be substantial fines levied by the rail authorities on the unreturned rail cars.

Even in the best of circumstances, this was a difficult process. Even more demanding was the fact that most of the military bases and secret cities lacked operable equipment of any type. Pieter had to comb the countryside, hiring dilapidated cranes to position just outside the restricted areas of the secret bases. The entire region surrounding these secret cities and bases had been taboo for so long that often Pieter could not persuade locals to go anywhere near them.

The tank cars arrived accompanied by the armed commando SWAT teams dispatched with each dismantlement shipment. Soon after the tank cars arrived, Pieter was informed that the base would not accept the delivery because the paperwork was not in order. "The Standoff" had begun.

When I arrived at my office in the United States that morning, I was briefed about the situation in Turinskaya, almost exactly on the other side of the world. For the next two days, a dialogue went back and forth between Pieter, on a satellite phone in Turinskaya, Sergey, in St. Petersburg, and I, in the United States. The only good news from the first day was that Pieter had been able to enter the base. Due to his prior Soviet Army Intelligence standing, he had managed to befriend the base commander.

The story that emerged reminded me of the legend about the Japanese soldier who was purportedly discovered in the 1980s on a remote Pacific island, unaware that World War II was over and quite happy believing it was still going on. The Turinskaya base commander was a dyed-in-the-wool Soviet and had devised the paperwork ruse as a bureaucratic attempt to prevent the delivery.

The truth was that the base commander was not at all happy about the collapse of the Soviet Union and was determined not to disarm or defuel his missiles. He believed the disarmament treaty was an American ploy. This guy sounded like a direct descendant of Stalin himself. It brought no end of comfort knowing that this guy, and probably many others like him, was empowered with intercontinental nuclear strike capability. The more I learned about the Soviet nuclear arsenal and its keepers, the less soundly I slept at night.

By the third day, we were still at an impasse. Never mind the international incident aspect, we were about to incur whopping fines for the delayed return of the rail cars. Given the number of rail cars in Turinskaya, we were looking at tens of thousands of dollars in charges if this standoff continued.

The fourth morning Sergey called with the story of how Pieter had worked some real magic over the past few days. Pieter was as engaging and funny a man as you would ever meet. Via no less than two bottles of vodka, he had convinced his new friend the base commander to relent.

Amazingly, accommodation was not the solution here. This was a Soviet loyalist, and Pieter had slowly brought the guy into the post–cold war era. Three days, two bottles of vodka, dozens of Pieter's very best jokes, and stories of the fine Americans Pieter had met finally turned the tide. I'm fairly certain that an account of my admonishment of Lenin was not among those stories.

I mention this incident in this context just to show that a quid pro quo is not always necessary. Sometimes, but rarely, a good, old-fashioned, reasoned position can carry the day. Other than the vodka, not a ruble or dollar changed hands.

KGB Face-off:
A Lesson in Saving International Face

The inland water route that runs south from St. Petersburg is called the Volga Baltic waterway. It comprises a system of rivers, reservoirs, and canals linking the Baltic Sea to the longest river in Europe, the Volga. Known as Mother Volga, the river is as intrinsic to Russian folklore as the mighty Mississippi is to American folklore. It originates near Moscow and flows 2,300 miles into a wide delta near Astrakhan into the Caspian Sea. Had word gotten out about the embroiled, high-level situation we stumbled into there, it would have added another rich story to the folklore about Mother Volga. While the first CTR incident transpired over a few days, the second occupied our attention for weeks.

Several small, PT-type boats were to be delivered to the Kazak Navy in the Kazak Caspian Sea port of Octau. They were outfitted with special gun mounts, for the function of the boats was to patrol the Caspian coastline preventing any nuclear, biological, or chemical weapons making their way to Iran. As evidence and verification of the KGB scrutiny we all assumed our office-to-office communications were under, there developed quite a brouhaha between the Russian KGB and the Kazakhstan government.

As we later pieced the story together, the KGB had known these vessels were arriving from the United States for transit across Russian soil—in reality into Russian *waters*. Evidently, the KGB was not happy about it and had developed a plan of interdiction. The boats had been loaded directly from the ocean-going vessels that brought them from the States onto a barge in St. Petersburg. The barge had then set sail on the 2300-mile passage on the Volga to the Russian town of Astrakhan. In Astrakhan, where the Volga empties into the Caspian Sea, the boats were transferred onto an Azeri barge for the transit to the Kazak naval base. The Azeri-owned barge was required because Kazak vessels were not allowed in Russian waters.

In Astrakhan, the boats were not loaded directly as they had been in St. Petersburg but were first set in the water. This was when the circumstances graduated from normal to absolutely haywire. Placing the Kazak boats in the Russian water violated the decree that Kazak vessels could not enter Russian waters. Even worse, these were Kazak *military* vessels, an even greater offense.

The KGB had been waiting patiently for just such an occurrence. Within minutes of being placed in the water, the boats were seized.

My company was instantaneously embroiled in an international incident involving three governments and countless spy agencies. It was somewhat amazing to me the incident did not make the newspapers. Sergey was as anxious as I had ever seen him. He was in constant contact with the KGB in St. Petersburg, which was relaying information straight from the Kremlin in Moscow. The situation lasted for two very long weeks. Yeltsin himself, it was said, was the ultimate decision maker in allowing the boats to be released back to our custody in Astrakhan.

We were not privy to what accommodation was made, if any, or what the negotiations might have entailed. For sure though, there were significant face issues at play in the loftiest levels of both the Russian and Kazak governments. Certainly the Russians had been embarrassed by the presence of prohibited Kazak naval vessels in their waters. The release of the vessels spoke volumes that a face saving resolution had been reached. Intrinsically, it was cultural.

Sign of the Times

In addition to the CTR contract, my company won two other newspaper headline-making contracts. One involved a Department of Energy program to modernize the decaying nuclear reactors, such as the infamous one in Chernobyl, in Russia and Ukraine, while the other was a State Department Berlin-style airlift campaign to help the tens of thousands refugees of the Chechen conflict. In those heady days, if there were headlines in the world news involving Russia, you could be fairly certain that my company was operating in the background.

Bosnian Accord:
A Lesson in Tap Dancing

Through our State Department contracts, we had been introduced to another state contractor, Military Professional Resources International (MPRI), based in Virginia. It was through MPRI that we began our involvement in the Bosnia program.

After the Dayton Accords, MPRI was hired by the newly created Federation to operate what was called the Train and Equip Program. This multinational-funded program had dual aspirations. One was to force the Bosnian Croats and Muslims, which comprised the two parts of the Federation, to work together. The other, and most pressing, desire was to create a military balance to secure a lasting peace between the Federation and the Bosnian Serb Republic, these being the two entities comprising the Republic of Bosnia and Herzegovina, as outlined by the Dayton Agreements.

The Dayton Accords attempted to take historical and ethnic boundaries and piece them together in an agreement that created a single state, yet allowed for self determination within each region of the three warring factions. Basically, the Dayton Accords was an attempt at a solution to a Rubik's Cube situation.

By the fall of 1996, the Republic of Bosnia and Herzegovina had been established and the Train and Equip Program was underway. Approximately $100 million in defense equipment, including rifles, machine guns, tanks, heavy artillery, armored personnel carriers, antitank weapons, and helicopters, was to be delivered over the next year. My company was hired to supervise the unloading of this equipment in the Bosnian port of Ploce. Additionally, the various logistical duties included the inventory of equipment and inland transit to military warehouses established in the Federation. An essential component of our task was to also separate the weapons from the ordnance and ammunition. As a precaution to assure cooperation between the Croats and Muslims, the weapons were to go to a warehouse in one part of the Federation while the ammunition and ordnance went to another.

The four-person team I sent to Ploce was there for over a month receiving and distributing the first ship of military equipment for the Federation. Another vessel was not expected for months, so my team returned to the United States.

As is typically the case in any underdeveloped area, not to mention one that has recently been war-ravaged for a number of years, any hint of business or money to be made brings out all types of suitors. In this case, the services surrounding the unloading and delivery of the military equipment was probably one of the largest pieces of business in the new country.

We were told that one of the powerful suitors was a Bosnian Muslim named Cengic. He had attained military hero status within the Federation for his efforts in gaining Iranian arms assistance during the conflict. But, Cengic was on the outs with the United States precisely because of his Iranian connections. As a matter of fact, the Train and Equip Program had been delayed for months until all military and intelligence relationships between Bosnia and Iran had been severed.

Later that year, another ship arrived. This time we were not contracted to perform the logistics services. In a surprising move, the Federation attaches had usurped the MPRI sub-contracting authority and had placed the logistics services elsewhere. Upon further investigation, I learned the logistics work was going to companies of "family and friends," and that those companies were purportedly owned by Cengic. This was an important revelation since it was widely understood that Cengic's past influence with Iran meant that he wasn't to be involved with the U.S. weapons and equipment in any way.

The instant I received this news I realized we were now squarely in a situation rife with face implications and definite accommodation overtones. Thinking about the situation, I saw it was clear that an accommodation in this instance would be a violation of the Foreign Corrupt Practices Act. Yet, any approach to the Federation attaches directly referencing the Cengic connection would be fruitless and probably serve to entrench the situation. Essentially, such action required cornering them in a fashion remarkably similar to that of my earlier dealings with the Harvard-educated Saudi.

I thought about the best line of approach. The Cengic issue was so politically charged that I knew the angle, but who to make the case to? I knew that MPRI had a very good relationship with the U.S. Ambassador to Bosnia and Herzegovina, James Pardew Jr. and I concluded that was the place to make my case, if I could get an audience.

I telephoned a senior MPRI official, Bob, and explained my ideas on how to deal with the situation. Bob was aware of the problem and was sympathetic. The last ship unloading had not gone well. Bob knew Ambassador Pardew quite well and offered to make the introduction.

We met at the Ambassador's office at the State Department. Pardew, fiftyish with a military bearing, listened attentively as I laid out the facts, how I came to know them, and how they all appeared to connect to Cengic. I chose my words carefully.

With tacit disclosure, I very generally sketched the issue of what might be transpiring regarding a quid pro quo and the uselessness of any direct confrontation by my company. As I tap-danced around the implied issues, Pardew merely nodded. When he spoke, the ambassador also chose his words carefully. I was impressed with the caliber of guy who was handling this powder keg area of the world. It was perhaps the most powerfully "pregnant" meeting I had ever been in. Nothing specific was said, but everything was understood.

The issue struck home, as I had hoped it would. While being carefully noncommittal, Pardew promised he would look into the whole situation on his next visit to Bosnia later that month. The Ambassador and I agreed that my company should continue our lobbying efforts with the Federation attachés just as before, without divulging any knowledge of a Cengic connection. Lastly, we would reveal nothing about our meeting.

After Pardew's visit to Bosnia, we received word from the Federation attaches that they wished to discuss contracting our services for the next ships. After lengthy talks with the Federation, we were reinstated as the logistical support contractor.

Pardew obviously impacted the result. I'm certain he raised the issues the United States had with any appearance of a Cengic connection. After all, that was his job as Ambassador. Since we were still soliciting the Federation attaches without having to tread on the volatile face-provoking issue, my company remained an unobjectionable option.

I had come a long way since the experience with the Harvard-educated Saudi businessman and my first introduction to the concept of saving face. Had I gone about the Bosnian situation differently, and had face become an issue, my company would have never reacquired the Federation contract.

A CIA Complaint:
A Lesson in Playing on an Uneven Field

The sale of my company was consummated in November 1996. The foothold I was able to forge in Russia and the New Republics was the primary asset the principle buyer, William Simon & Sons (the same Simon that was the Secretary of Treasury under Reagan), coveted enough to fork over cash and stock valued at somewhere over thirty million dollars.

The lessons I had learned in my globetrotting career were instrumental to the success we had in the NIS. What I couldn't know at the time of the sale, was just how crucial these same lessons would become to my achievements in dealing with the aftermath of the sale.

A major focus in early 1997 was a contract for the modernization of a paper mill in Russia west of the Urals. I'll leave the actual mill unidentified for reasons that will become imminently clear. I will simply refer to it as the Nizhny Mill. The word *nizhny* means "lower" or "below" in Russian, and everything about this caper fits with the connotations of those words.

I only allowed my company to do business with a Russian or CIS business entity if we were guaranteed a loan or grant from a Western institution—an institution such as the World Bank, the European Bank for Reconstruction and Development (EBRD), or a governmental institution like the United States Export Import (Ex-Im) Bank. This ensured the CIS business entity had hard currency to pay for services.

The funding source for the purchasing and shipment of the equipment to renovate the Russian mill was the U.S. Ex-Im Bank. The Ex-Im loaned money to the mill, collateralized by future mill earnings made possible by the renovation. In making the loan to the mill, the Ex-Im Bank paid the money for the equipment directly to the U.S. corporation selling the equipment. I'll call the U.S. company in this matter the A&B Company.

My ace sales rep, Debbie, no longer working on her Russian, had made contact with the appropriate managers at A&B Company. She arranged a meeting and subsequently briefed me on the situation.

Debbie explained that A&B Company was not in charge of the transport decision. That decision was made by the *Russians* running the mill. One final note of significance was added during her meeting; the Russians were already speaking to a German company about the equipment deliveries.

I called Sergey to explain the situation, and he, in turn, promised to call the mill director immediately to arrange a meeting. When I heard back from Sergey after his visit to the Nizhny Mill, he described the perilous scenario. The Russian director had barely given Sergey the time of day before conveying to Sergey, in very "Russian" terms, his preference for the German company. Sergey summed it up by telling me that the director's pocket had already made the decision. This was a term I had heard Sergey use before, and I understood that an accommodation had been made.

This was not good. I knew we were entering a new and dangerous sales arena. The reason had to do with the prohibitions of the U.S. Foreign Corrupt Practices Act (FCPA). The playing field the FCPA created for Americans competing for business overseas was terribly uneven. The FCPA made it illegal for my company, or even for Sergey as a representative of my company, to make any type of payment, bribery really, to the director of the mill. The Germans had no such restriction.

I was forced by the very real threat of jail to come to terms with the fact that a shipping contract guaranteed by a U.S. government agency, bought from a U.S. manufacturer, could not possibly be legally won by a U.S. firm. A German competitor, or for that matter a Canadian, British, French, Dutch, Japanese, Korean, etc. had no such legal problems competing for this U.S. government-financed business.

How could this be? The Act is aimed at bribery committed for the sole purpose of influencing business. Payments to decision makers as a quid pro quo were expressly illegal for U.S. citizens, for U.S. companies, or even for the representatives of U.S. companies.

I admit I fully understand the ethical point of the act. I'm all for it. The practical reality was that the ethical point made the U.S. financed business off limits to U.S. businesses. That wrinkle was very difficult to accept. Pursuing the shipping contract for the Nizhny Mill would be futile—kind of like bringing a water pistol to a gun fight.

Any American competing for business overseas needs to understand, and comply with, the FCPA. Understanding what comprises the illegal portion of accommodation and what doesn't is very important. You won't like it any better than I do, but you need to know it.

A coincidental meeting occurred soon after this incident. In March, on St. Patrick's Day to be exact, an attractive lady in her mid to late thirties arrived in my office. Her first name was Katherine, and she was impeccably dressed. We shook hands and exchanged business cards. Her card looked exactly like the card of a public relations company. In a way, public relations was what she did, but her true employer was a surprise. She worked for the Central Intelligence Agency (CIA).

As we sat down, she explained her reason for meeting with me. The CIA tried to take advantage of the fact that American business people working in political hotspots like Bosnia and Russia might inadvertently happen across helpful intelligence information. It was her job to be a contact source for those companies willing to assist. Katherine explained that, in many situations, business executives didn't realize what might constitute beneficial intelligence. She said she would appreciate it if I would call whenever I remotely thought I had anything of interest. In a way, I was being "deputized." What else could I say but "sure"?

Before the meeting ended, Katherine asked if she could relay any complaints I had through her channels. I thought for a moment. Did I *ever* have a complaint she could relay. I told her about the Nizhny situation.

I was not surprised when she told me that, of all the complaints she heard from American business people competing overseas, the inequities of the FCPA was the most frequent.

Sign of the Times

In fairness to U.S. legislators there have been attempts to level the playing field. The United States is a member of the Organization for Economic Cooperation and Development (OECD) along with thirty other countries including Britain, France, Germany, Japan, Korea, and Sweden—basically all the major economic players in the world.

In February 1999, the OECD Convention on Combating Bribery of Foreign Public Officials went into effect. The purpose of the convention was to make it a crime, under the laws of *all* the signatory countries, for citizens from signatory countries to bribe foreign officials. Well, it was a great thought, and U.S. legislators had given it the old college try in order to level the playing field. However, the impact of the OECD convention had a very limited effect.

According to the U.S. Department of State's "Fact Sheet of June 29, 2001: Major Findings on Report of OECD Anti-Bribery Pact," from May of 2000 to April 30, 2001 there were allegations that sixty-one contracts worth $37 billion may have been affected by bribery. Of these, U.S. firms were believed to have lost nine contracts worth $4 billion. Firms from countries signatory to the convention accounted for 70 percent of allegations. Further, it stated the U.S. State Department had not been aware of *any* prosecutions by countries party to the OECD convention. More recent findings have not changed significantly. Has the playing field been leveled? I think not.

A Mafia Murder from London:
A Lesson in Loss

I had never been to a Russian Old New Year celebration, and, to bring in 1997, Sergey was throwing a big one. It was held at a restaurant along the Neve River in the heart of St. Petersburg. What a party it turned out to be. I have never, ever seen so many people party all night and into the following morning—and the amount of vodka consumed was nothing short of astonishing. As I staggered out of the restaurant that morning, bidding everyone a Happy Old New Year, I exchanged well wishes with Sergei Vdovin. It was the last time I saw him.

Later that summer, Sergey and I met in London for our monthly meeting. The administrative "to dos" had begun to pile up so quickly that they required we get together at least once each month. We took to meeting in Europe, as it was approximately halfway for each of us. It also gave us an opportunity to enjoy the cities of Europe for a couple of days each time we met.

On the second night of a July meeting in London, we took a cab to the financial district near Parliament. Sergey and I enjoyed almost all the same foods, and our favorite was sushi. The concierge in our hotel had recommended the restaurant where we were headed on that cool, beautiful summer evening.

The atmosphere all day had been subdued due to a perplexing situation with Vdovin, Sergey's longtime friend and our joint partner. Late the first night of our meeting, Sergey had received a call on his mobile phone from Vdovin's wife. She told Sergey that Vdovin had not yet arrived home or called that night. It was already well past one o'clock in the morning in St. Petersburg.

This was not overly concerning. Vdovin often acted much younger than his thirty-two years, so we were not worried until the following morning when we still had no word of him at home or at work. Through the day, we were able to piece together bits of information regarding Vdovin's activities the prior day. The information was foreboding. A friend, Glaseri, had seen Vdovin pulled over to the side of a deserted road talking to two men, neither of whom Glaseri had ever seen before. Within minutes, Glaseri received a call on his mobile phone from Vdovin who asked Glaseri to return and give him assistance with the two men. When Glaseri reached the deserted road where Vdovin's car had been, no one was there.

That night, during our sushi dinner, Sergey called each hour to get an update on any news of Vdovin. His mobile phone wouldn't work from the subterranean recesses of the fabulous sushi restaurant so Sergey excused himself to go up to the street to place each call. Finishing dinner, I waited for the check. Sergey went ahead of me to place his third call of the evening.

I paid the bill and stepped outside into the lovely London evening just as Sergey finished his call. He looked at me and just shook his head, indicating there was no news. From his demeanor, I could see the situation was weighing heavily on him. He was obviously very worried. For the first time since we learned of Vdovin's disappearance, Sergey was totally disconsolate.

Sergey and I left London the following morning with no word from or about Vdovin. We knew something was very wrong. Never before had he been out of touch for such an extended period. The sighting by Glaseri increasingly came to have ominous overtones, and we weren't prepared for the reality.

After I arrived back in the United States, the call came during the early morning hours. Vdovin was dead. He had been found in a garbage dump behind some apartments. His body had been inserted headfirst into a large bag, and he had been shot six times in the head.

Lying in bed, I was gripped with a sense of foreboding that, even to this day, I have difficulty describing. I had never been close to anyone who had died violently. Moreover, I had never been anywhere close to a murder, not to mention a homicide with all the earmarks of a Mafia hit, and that's what this certainly was. Needless to say, I didn't sleep for the remainder of the night.

I arrived very early at the office and called Sergey. He was not himself. I was able to exchange thoughts about why this had occurred. As in the Barry situation in Almaty three years before, the important and pressing question that came to mind was had the murder been personal or business? The widespread Mafia situation in Russia made this classic *Godfather* line very meaningful and entirely appropriate. We couldn't ignore the possibility that this was a warning. If that were the case, serious steps would need to be taken.

Also, Sergey did not expect the police to be much help in apprehending whoever had committed the murder. In matters with such obvious Mafia overtones as this, Sergey explained the police did not expend much in the manner of investigation—only perfunctory and rudimentary inquiries were made. These were the legal practicalities.

We required expert assistance to effectively deal with the problems or potential threats and to mount a concerted effort to solve the crime. In this environment, we chose to hire a private security firm with tentacles reaching far into both worlds of police and Mafia. The obvious choice was Lennox, a firm we had developed a good relationship with for the armed transit of shipments.

That morning we also discussed the funeral arrangements. Per Russian Orthodox custom, funeral ceremonies were to be held the very next day. This fact made the question of my attending the funeral a moot point. If I took a flight that very night, I would still not arrive in time to attend. What would have been a huge security issue did not need to be addressed. The security for Sergey was quite complex, and my presence would have entailed something akin to a head of state security detail.

To my relief, the funeral and interment passed without incident. The grief and sadness was palpable even from six thousand miles away. I was told the sight of Vdovin's wife and child was more than any of the attendees could bear. Beyond the issue of personal safety, not having to witness this heart-wrenching scene made me ever so grateful for my inability to attend.

It had not yet been twenty-four hours since I learned the terrible news. It seemed as if the entire world was turned on its edge, and I had somehow fallen into a cold war thriller. The sense of doom and foreboding increased in the coming days.

The day after the funeral, a manager came to my office to relate a deeply disturbing rumor that suggested the crime was business-related. A U.S. representative of a steamship company, one possessing a major presence in the Port of St. Petersburg, told my manager that the rumor circulating in the port was that the murder of Vdovin had been a warning to scale back the operations and growing influence of my company. The steamship representative explained that the reasoning behind the rumor was that the second in command had been killed to serve as a warning.

I called Sergey and relayed the story to him. He was not aware of the rumor, and I saw that as definitely a good thing. Sergey vowed to immediately convey the rumor to Lennox. The next morning—only the fourth since the discovery of Vdovin's body—Sergey called to explain that Lennox could not confirm or deny the rumor. They would need a few days, maybe more, in order to offer any concrete investigative results.

A security detail was assigned by Lennox to the building lobby and to the floor where our offices were located. The personal security measures that had been recommended for Sergey were elaborate. He had been assigned an armed escort who was also to be his full-time driver. This escort was a former Soviet special forces type and very highly trained. Additionally, Sergey's personal security for the immediate future included an armed perimeter escort, unidentified and unknown to both him and to his driver escort. This precaution was to avoid either Sergey or the driver inadvertently giving up the perimeter security. Needless to say, the perimeter escort was of the same special forces background and training. If anyone were to attempt to harm Sergey, they would be met with lethal force from two highly capable sources.

Finally, after three weeks Lennox told Sergey, and even the police, that they were 90 percent certain that Vdovin's murder had been personal. Unfortunately, this information offered no certainty. Believe me, 90 percent sounds like an insignificant probability when total assurance is the only acceptable conclusion. Consequently, we felt very little sense of relief. The murder hung like a dark cloud around the offices both in the United States and Russia.

From a problem-solving standpoint, even with all the resources and effort that had been thrown at the situation, we had made little tangible headway. The answers were all couched in "maybe" or "probably." Sometimes that's the way it is—problems and answers don't always fit neatly together

In the weeks following the murder, Sergey and I spoke only sparingly about our personal theories developing around the investigations. I knew he would not want to discuss these subjects by telephone. This was a long understanding between us. Sergey, in the first year of our partnership, had explained that most Russians believed the government monitored all international phone calls and that this practice had not ended with the fall of the Soviet Union. It was an urban legend, of course, but it was a fervently held belief.

It was for this reason, among others, that we met each month to talk. In late August, I met with Sergey in Amsterdam a week later than originally planned. Sergey had postponed the original date for our meeting due to a Russian Orthodox custom—it would have been a major transgression for Sergey to miss the sacred event planned for the forty day remembrance of Sergei Vdovin.

I knew in this monthly meeting that I would receive a detailed update on the investigations, ours and the official one. In Amsterdam, I learned that there were two personal issues that had surfaced that were believed to contain the answer to the murder mystery. The two theories that Sergey conveyed to me for the first time were both plausible, yet quite disparate.

The first theory involved an altercation Vdovin had in a Moscow nightclub some months before. Vdovin was a bit drunk and made advances toward an attractive woman on the dance floor. She told Vdovin that she was with her boyfriend, but he would not relent. Her boyfriend apparently saw Vdovin chatting up his girlfriend and made his way over to where they were standing. The story, as told by one of our Moscow employees who was with Vdovin that night, had it that sharp words ensued. Suddenly, and apparently without provocation, Vdovin took a swing and decked the boyfriend. Before the dispute turned into a brawl, the usual burly bouncers found in places like this came out of nowhere and collared the two.

Vdovin had made a transgression right out of 1920s Chicago. The boyfriend was a well-known gangster in Moscow, and the nightclub was just as notorious as a gangster hangout. As the bouncers held the irate gangster at bay, he made an ominous vow, was heard by all, that Vdovin would soon be dead. Those gathered around the altercation were instantly hushed by the threat. Most knew of the gangster, and his street reputation had it that he was a violent man.

Vdovin was ushered out of the nightclub. Those who were there said the crowd stared at him as if he were the proverbial dead man walking. It was felt Vdovin had just received a death sentence and was exiting the club with one foot already planted in the grave.

Even though the murder had taken place in St. Petersburg, this theory had some validity. It would explain the two men who were unknown to Glaseri, and it accounted for the money that had *not* been taken from Vdovin's body. It could also explain the execution style of the murder.

The problem with the theory, though, was *also* the money—the money that was not stolen and that seemed to be the center of Vdovin's very odd behavior and actions in the days before the crime. In retrospect, Sergey was certain Vdovin's strange behavior before his death held the answer to the question of whether the murder was business or personal.

To explain this second theory and his logic, Sergey recounted events from the past year regarding Vdovin's emerging lifestyle and circle of friends. In Russian terms, both Sergey and Vdovin were doing quite well financially. Vdovin, being much younger than his years, flaunted his money on high-priced European cars and a lavish lifestyle. Additionally, he was investing money into refurbishing old apartment buildings.

This type of investment was actually a smart move—one many Russians with excess income were engaged in. The new commercialism running rampant in Russia was bringing far more Westerners to live there, and acceptable living quarters were in very short supply. A decently renovated apartment with washer, dryer, shower and individual heating was bringing huge rents from the corporations desperate to house their executives.

Sergey learned by happenstance that Vdovin had transgressed, by virtue of his refurbishing investments, into an area of association that law-abiding Russians avoided like the plague. He learned that Vdovin was renting to, partying with, and investing with known elements of the St. Petersburg Mafia.

Sergey had taken his daughter to school one morning before going to the office. Arriving later than customary, Sergey walked into the office to find one of the most notorious gangsters of the St. Pete Mafia casually lounging in the visitor area. Evidently, this guy often frequented the front pages of the local newspapers and was a pseudo-celebrity. The picture in my head, as Sergey described the encounter, was as if I had walked into my office and found Tony Soprano waiting.

The Russian Soprano was there to meet Vdovin, who was late as usual. Vdovin finally arrived and met with the gangster for nearly an hour. After the mobster left the office, Sergey demanded Vdovin explain the reasons for this most unwelcome visit. Vdovin explained his apartment refurbishment connection with the gangster and said that he had become a good friend.

That encounter had been approximately one year before Vdovin's death, and there had been no more visits to the office by gangsters. Vdovin had not spoken of his associations with them again. His murder, although, brought that encounter back to disturbing prominence.

Sergey continued stating that, just one week prior to the murder, an unusual series of events unfolded. For some unspoken reason, Vdovin suddenly decided to sell his five series BMW. He was overheard making hurried sale arrangements from his desk at the office. It was obvious that Vdovin needed money for something, and he needed it fast. Within a day or so, he sold the car for far, far less than the going market price.

Additionally, and, in twenty-twenty hindsight, the oddest of his actions, Vdovin had gone to Sergey and pleaded for a loan of tens of thousands of dollars. Taken aback, Sergey inquired as to the reason for the loan, and Vdovin gave an unconvincing song and dance about a really hot investment opportunity. Although very skeptical and a bit apprehensive, Sergey gave Vdovin the few thousand dollars that he had immediately available. Three days later, Vdovin was found murdered with the money from the sale of the BMW and the money Sergey had loaned him still on his body.

Again, if the second theory was accepted, then why was the money left? There were no good answers except, possibly, that it was left to deflect suspicion. It would not have been a substantial amount of money to these types anyway.

Both theories had credible points. Not quite following Sergey's logic regarding the second theory and its relation to the crime, I asked which theory he felt was most probable. Sergey replied concisely that either could be true, but that we would almost certainly never know. What he was sure of, and why he had offered the explanation concerning the Russian Tony Soprano, was that Vdovin's embrace of the Mafia lifestyle was the prime contributor, in one way or another, to his death. Sergey believed that what was important was Vdovin's behavior in the days before the crime. He was certain beyond a doubt that a warning had been issued to Vdovin and that the warning had resulted in the very peculiar and hurried behavior.

I realized Sergey's logic was offering the kind of assurance we had been seeking regarding the personal or business nature of the crime. While Sergey would have dearly loved to solve the crime, both Lennox and the police had stressed the futility of that desire. So, the best we could hope for was some assurance the crime did not involve a warning to the company. Hence, Sergey and I were not in any danger.

In Sergey's logic the law of the land had been followed. A warning had been issued, and Vdovin's actions were in response to that warning. As Sergey told me years before, when the third warning comes, no one is left to tell about it.

The logic, in context with understanding the law of the land, provided the only solace possible from the sordid affair. The issue was personal. Thus, business could continue without the fear of additional incidents.

The murder remains unsolved to this day.

Cultural Snapshot

The Russian Orthodox religion teaches that the spirit of the deceased remains on earth for forty days before departing. According to tradition, the soul of the dead finally leaves the earth on the fortieth day and ascends to heaven or descends to hell, thus calling for special prayers. This tradition is based upon the belief that Jesus, on the fortieth day after Resurrection—Easter to us, Holy Pascha to the Orthodox—ascended into Heaven to make a place for the rest of us.

In modern day terms, on the fortieth day after leaving the realm of the living the spirit's departure is cause for a major celebration by relatives and close friends. Well wishes, toasts, and fond remembrances of the deceased mark the occasion. The Russian Orthodox believe the spirit takes part in this final celebration and then departs for the afterlife.

It seems to me such an uplifting and joyous cultural rite for the commemoration of a life.

Afghan Surprise:
A Lesson in Extreme Deception

Vdovin's murder, with all its tension and stress, engendered a bout of major soul searching on my part. I was desperately unhappy with the culture being developed by the new owners of my company, and Vdovin's murder put that unhappiness into brilliant perspective. Very simply put, life can be too short. So, I left the company and was on the sidelines for a bit over three years.

Ending that hiatus in 2001, my career entered into the stage of my third entrepreneurial adventure. I rehired the best and brightest of my old staff and formed a new company called Logenix. The plans to start Logenix were finalized just before the attacks of September 11. The upheaval of the business environment after the terrorist attacks certainly gave us cause to pause in deciding whether to carry out our plans for Logenix.

Like so many other times in my business career, intuition was the factor providing the resolve to move forward. I had a sense that the United States' response to this unprecedented attack on our homeland might yield opportunities that could involve me in the most interesting and important undertakings of my life. So, defying the prevalent commercial wisdom of the time, I jumped headfirst into the turbulent business environment of the immediate post-9/11 United States. I couldn't have known just how profoundly intuitive my sense would turn out to be. In just a little over three years, Logenix attained growth and industry recognition rivaling that of the heady post-Soviet days.

During this time I encountered acute experiences that gave real context to demonstrating the significance and importance of my lessons. The Abu Ghraib situation described earlier could be viewed as an extreme outcome of the failure to grasp the cultural forces existent in Iraq. In a similar way the following insights, gained from the most dangerous areas I have ever been involved in, represent what could be viewed as the improbable outer boundaries regarding the respective lessons. As the experiences will reveal, the outer boundaries were not so improbable and the resultant ripple impact of each of these situations had tsunami-like effects. I said we would get back to Iraq, and that road leads through Afghanistan.

The war to evict the Taliban and eradicate al Qaeda was successfully waged, and within months the U.S. government began the rebuilding of Afghanistan. Just like darn near every other major hotspot over the past twenty years, I was involved. Prime among the initial infrastructure efforts was a program, implemented on behalf of Da Afghanistan Bank, to print and circulate new currency while also collecting and destroying old currency. The driving reason, as I understood it, was to remove any and all financial ability the Taliban and/or al Qaeda might have to continue operations.

For one reason or other, the U.S. government was in a very big hurry to begin the currency conversion process. I had never before or since seen the U.S. government, an entity renowned for its procedural plodding, in such haste.

From the very beginning of the currency operation, it was evident that the U.S. representatives in Kabul were relying heavily on both information and guidance from personnel at the United Nations Joint Logistics Center (UNJLC)—especially from a fellow we'll call Mick. Mick, for all intents the proxy for the U.S. officials, was essentially directing the contracting actions. Hence, communication with Mick at UNJLC in Kabul was substantive and open.

The problematic area of gearing up the currency program turned out to be contracting for airplanes and helicopters, which was my company's responsibility. What should have been a fairly straightforward detail was complicated by an unusual requirement from the U.S. officials overseeing the program. This requirement stipulated that the flight operations and security could not be under the supervision of either U.N. or Coalition Forces.

Why the U.S. officials would adopt this curious stand was perplexing for two main reasons. First of all, we discovered it was highly irregular for an aircraft to operate in any world "hot zone," —and Afghanistan certainly qualified in that category—without being overseen by one or the other. Second, and most odd, a guy from the U.N. was essentially directing the operations. It seemed operating under the supervision of the U.N. would be very simple to arrange. The reasoning behind the contracting requirements came to light only after a bizarre series of events occurring over a two-month period.

Anecdotally, the security concerns dominating the affair were put into unique perspective by one of the Eastern European aircraft owners with whom I spoke. In his very thickly accented English he summarized our request, "Let me to understand. You wish for former Soviet pilots to fly around Afghanistan with millions of money with not security from Coalition Forces or U.N. You are funny guy. I must tell this to all my Russian friends!"

During the course of the initial, and unusual, three weeks of the helicopter contracting my company had an early bid by a Russian helicopter company—I'll call them Russkie Aviation—rejected by U.S. officials. Ostensibly, the rejection was due to an inability to mobilize quickly enough. After the initial bid by Russkie Aircraft was rejected, we obtained approximately ten other bids from companies throughout Eastern Europe. Each and every one of these other bidding companies were, within days of their bids, refused permission to operate in Afghanistan by their respective country's Civil Aeronautics Authority (CAA). And, in each and every case, the lack of Coalition or U.N. flight security oversight was the reason for the denial.

The initial Russkie bid would have gone unnoticed save for the fact that, only weeks later, a second bid by the very same Russkie Aviation was accepted—by the very same U.S. officials—at over double the original bid. Clever negotiating! Obviously, the negotiation for the helicopter services had not gone as expected.

All in all, we just couldn't make sense of Russkie's bid doubling. At the time, I remember thinking that the negotiation had been a bit like Howard's situation with the babushka hats—at least to the extent that we thought we had been in a position of leverage, but had misunderstood the leverage for some as yet unknown reason.

The contracting for the airplane was even stranger, if that's possible to imagine. In a series of events that began with a letter from the UNJLC—a letter that at first glance appeared to grant oversight from the U.N. for the airplane operations—the situation went from the improbable to the absurd.

A Ukrainian registered aircraft, an AN-32, would ultimately depart from Kiev for Kabul with a CAA official onboard. The aircraft had only been given preliminary authority to operate due to that ambiguous UNJLC letter. A Ukrainian CAA official accompanied the aircraft to Afghanistan as a verification procedure. The inspector would verify the security arrangements and, all being as suggested by the UNJLC letter, quickly be on his way back to the Ukraine.

The AN-32 landed in Kabul only to find none of the apparent security promises of the UNJLC letter to be factual—most importantly, the promise of U.N. oversight did not exist. Through a series of translated meetings the Ukrainians were given the distinct impression that their presence in Kabul was not welcome and the UNJLC letter was dismissed as irrelevant. It became clear to me that all of the ingredients of an irresolvable face issue were developing.

On the second morning after the arrival of the AN-32, we received grim news. The Ukrainian Ministry of Defense had issued a stern communiqué demanding the immediate return of the AN-32, its crew, and the inspector. The Ukrainian "Pentagon" was actually involved.

After the Ukrainian aircraft departed Kabul, we received astonishing news regarding how events had transpired during that tense two-day period.

Upon arrival in Kabul, the Ukrainian crew was met by none other than the UNJLC fellow named Mick. He had been very involved in the helicopter search and was now equally involved in the airplane contracting. At first blush, Mick's presence did not seemed odd—until we learned that he was not there as a UNJLC representative. Oddly, Mick no longer worked for the UNJLC. He now worked for a private company that was to supply the flight management for both the helicopter and AN-32 aircraft operations.

At this point, to describe the developing events as strange would be quite an understatement. It would take some intensive scrutiny by my staff to piece together a fairly intricate web of chicanery.

The first of the discomforting news bits we uncovered was that Mick had either worked for or had some direct affiliation with Russkie Aviation in the not too distant past—the very same company that had doubled its price for the choppers. Next, we learned that the signature on the UNJLC letter—the letter that was squarely responsible for the bizarre airplane predicament—belonged to none other than Mick. Finally, the most distressing bit of news was that Mick had been the translator for all communications in the meetings between the U.S. officials and the Ukrainian AN-32 crew. How coincidentally convenient! Every peculiar turn in both contracting efforts seemed to have one thing in common—Mick.

The worst was yet to come. Over the next few days, I learned that the blame for the surreal aircraft affair was being placed squarely on my company. To try and comprehend the situation and find a workable solution, I needed to get a complete grasp of the issues first hand. I was off to the source.

Boarding the old Arianna Airlines plane in Dubai, I was amazed at just how tough-looking the Afghanis seated around me were. These guys were collectively much bigger than their Pakistani or Iranian neighbors, and their skin had the look of leather from a decades-old bomber jacket. Hands were gnarled and calloused. Teeth were either missing or the color of tree bark. These guys looked like they could walk straight up into the Himalayas and stay there for years without needing food or heavy clothing. Approaching Kabul, I gazed down upon the incredibly desolate mountains, somewhat in awe of the lunarlike landscape surrounding the Afghani capital. I was not in the least surprised the Soviets had failed to conquer these rugged people.

After landing and exiting the airport, I was met by our local agent to take me to the hotel. Finally, I was heeding my own travel lessons. The drive was an amazing weave through a nineteenth-century country devastated by twenty-five years of modern warfare. Buildings were in crumbled heaps everywhere. The mostly unpaved streets weaved capriciously meeting in badly crowded circular intersections. Autos, hand-pushed carts, and donkeys all crowded together fighting over the ever-diminishing right of way.

I immediately went to the operation center of the currency conversion project. Not surprisingly, nothing could have been at this point, the ops center was located in premises run by the company Mick now worked for. Against one wall of the cavernous room comprising the ops center, extending a good twelve feet from floor to ceiling and at least as wide, was an enormous map of Afghanistan. Nearby stood a row of desks comprising the flight ops management. There, I began the polite process of introducing myself. Occupying one of those desks was a fellow approximately six feet tall and dark haired—that was Mick.

Immediately after I introduced myself to Mick, he—without any noticeable change in demeanor—introduced me to officials from Da Afghan Bank. I exchanged pleasantries with them while they officiously studied the large map. I surmised that I should wait for a more private moment to see what additional information I might be able to garner from Mick. I then moved to the far end of the room.

Standing near a large window lighting that part of the room, were a number of American-looking persons—their style of dress was a dead giveaway. I introduced myself to a tall, grayish fellow with glasses. His eyes showed instant recognition at the mention of my company. He had barely said, "How do you do," before launching a verbal assault about the AN-32 issue and its departure. As his spiteful tirade gathered momentum, his teeth were clenched and veins were exploding from the sides of his temples. Not even as a child had I received such a public and disdainful tongue-lashing.

I stood there, not quite sure how to respond or react. I politely stammered rebuttals to his angry assertions to which came astoundingly uninformed replies. Within a minute or so, it became unmistakably apparent to me that this red faced, very cranky U.S. official knew not one thing about the hoaxish UNJLC letter, the security concerns, or any of the important circumstances surrounding either the arrival or the departure of the AN-32. The revelations rendered me numb.

I was getting a fairly good sense of the atmosphere that the Ukrainians must have had to deal with. Here I was being "dissed" quite publicly by a U.S. official who knew not one damn thing about the causes or effects of the situation. I'm sure my face was flushed, and my ears were red as beets.

I glanced across the room and saw good ole Mick, studiously ignoring my predicament, peering at the gigantic map of Afghanistan pinned to the wall. Suddenly, right there in the middle of the public whipping, all the pieces of the incongruous puzzle came together.

It was unfathomable this U.S. official knew nothing of the UNJLC letter or the security concerns inherent to the matter. While receiving our account of the meetings from the Ukrainian owner of the AN-32, we had been told the UNJLC letter had been the main topic of discussion. Mick *must* have done some creative translating in those meetings. There could be no other answer.

It also seemed no stretch to assume Mick had given every detail of the helicopter negotiations to the owner of Russkie Aviation. Talk about leverage. Given Mick's past relationship and his "coincidental" current employment, it became clear how that chopper bid had doubled. But, how did Russkie Aviation get CAA approval from the Russian government? Again, it seemed no stretch to assume that Mick most likely wrote another UNJLC letter.

With the verbal assault winding down, all the dots were connecting. It stood to reason that the strange circumstances giving rise to the whole sordid situation, the zealous intent to avoid Coalition or U.N. flight security, was probably Mick's doing as well. The entire Afghan currency conversion project had been compromised from the very outset.

As I reflected back on the bizarre affair, I was struck by the number of extreme outcomes—each one highlighting the significance of my lessons—that had presented themselves. The mystifying turns of the negotiations for the helicopter bid had resulted in a doubled bid by Russkie Aviation. The "DEFCON III" level of escalation by the Ukrainian Ministry of Defense, in an effort to save face, was due to the inestimable embarrassment the Ukrainian AN-32 crew and inspector must have felt upon such an unwelcome greeting in Kabul. Finally, the communications issue surrounding the UNJLC letter had become incredibly muddled due to the reliance on one translated opinion in a very important context. Had the U.S. officials been cognizant of my cultural lessons, the Afghan currency conversion project would have evolved very, very differently.

At the very least, these extreme circumstances should have been a reverberating signal to everyone to look a bit closer at the situation—and the main character. Even a cursory overview would surmise something underhanded was afoot. In this case, the culprit was wrapped in clothing provided by an unassailable, at least at that time, institution of world renown—the U.N. Knowing deceitfulness can come from supposedly irreproachable sources is important to keep in mind.

As for resolving the aircraft issue, once the U.S. government officials learned of the UNJLC letter—and especially of the author—they were chagrined, to say the least. My company was duly, yet without apology, relieved of any blame.

Saddam's Ruins:
A Lesson in Culture and Faulty Logic

Approaching the Baghdad Airport on a Royal Wings flight from Amman, my eyes were focused out the aircraft window, but not on the details that would normally preoccupy me. Usually during these approaches to a new area, especially one as intriguing as Baghdad, my rapt absorption was with the terrain and with searching out famous historical landmarks like the Tigris River. Not this time. I was peering uneasily for the giveaway exhaust trail of the much feared SAMs (surface to air missiles).

I had been expecting something similar to the corkscrew landing in Pakistan years before, yet the flight I was on was making a traditional low approach. I learned later that week that the turboprop aircraft that I arrived on did not present a hot enough heat profile to be effectively tracked by a SAM.

The tension level of the landing was a fitting introduction to the visit to Baghdad. Every car ride, almost every movement, was made with the specter of the potential of immediate and lethal danger. I had never been anywhere like this. Baghdad made Lagos seem like a veritable vacation oasis.

The arrivals hall, if you could call the semi-wrecked old storage facility located a mile from the actual Baghdad Airport terminal by such a term, was poorly lit and poorly air-conditioned. No one presented a visa to the U.S. soldiers manning what was loosely termed the immigration process.

Exiting the makeshift arrivals hall my Iraq country manager, Art, and I were met by the heavily armed personal security detail (PSD) I had arranged. Tommy, a young former Army Ranger was the chief of our security detail. LT, an Army veteran, was the battalion chief in charge of getting all arrivals safely to the Green Zone (GZ) or to the secured hotel. Both Tommy and LT were outfitted like SWAT team members— black body armor, M-14 automatic rifles, 9 mm pistols, and sophisticated communication equipment obvious by telltale earpiece/mouthpiece headgear. Consistent with their combat training, they carried their weapons in front of them, at the ready at all times. All of this, plus the fact they exuded a no-nonsense attitude really brought the violence potential into razor-sharp focus.

The SUV assigned to us pulled up. We piled in and began to exit the airport and the U.S. base that encompasses it, Camp Victory. I had expected to see a lot of military equipment, but the sheer numbers of weapons-mounted Hummers, Bradley fighting vehicles (BFVs), and M-1 Abrams battle tanks (MBTs) were still astonishing. Exiting the perimeter security around the airport, we turned onto the single most dangerous twelve kilometers in the world, the road from the airport to the GZ. In military parlance, we were on Route Irish.

The invasion and its magnitude became visible as we moved around Baghdad. We saw the Communications Ministry, or what remained of it, and many other Iraqi government buildings. Taking the Communications Ministry as example, not only had buildings near it been unaffected, but much of the ministry itself was intact. There had been a direct hit through the center, leaving the weird impression that the ministry had imploded into itself. Other government buildings, power plants, and Iraqi military installations all had the similar signature of the air campaign that had raged over Baghdad. The brutal power and efficiency of modern warfare was awe-inspiringly apparent.

Outside of the war ravages, Baghdad was not as modern as I had expected. It was very different from other major Arab capitals I had seen. I had expected something similar to the Ottoman-inspired mosques of Cairo's citadel or even the whitewashed Mediterranean modernism of Amman. What I saw was more along the lines of Soviet Moscow with palm trees.

Adding to the surreal effect of this oxymoronic visual hodgepodge were the "Texas Ts" lining the roadways as we approached the GZ. These approximately ten-foot-high concrete barriers lined both sides of the road all around the GZ to prevent vehicles from being subjected to rocket-propelled grenade (RPG) attacks. These barriers had a tunnel effect that made it almost impossible to get a sense of direction during the entire visit. Whenever we traveled outside the barriers, the absence of these same Texas Ts made us feel as if we were completely exposed.

The fortifications at the GZ were stunning. The approach to what became known as Suicide Gate was a hundred meter S-weave through cement barricades. As the vehicle approached the entry, off to the left of the archway a BFV trained its guns directly on us. In front, a MBT pointed its menacing 120 mm cannon in our direction. A soldier approached our vehicle, gun at the ready, and asked our reasons for access. Given the extreme danger he faced on a minute-by-minute basis, I was impressed with the soldier's steady politeness.

We passed through the checkpoint and felt an easing of tension as we entered the relatively safe confines of the GZ. We were on our way to the Convention Center (CC) located just next to the infamous Al Rasheed Hotel.

We were there to meet with U.S. government personnel that, at that time, occupied offices in the CC.

After the unnerving impact of the plethora of strange visual images that greeted us, the scene in and around the CC was somewhat normal, albeit most normal offices do not include dozens of heavily armed men casually lounging around reception areas. Our meetings in the CC went well, and we drove over to the gargantuan example of excess that the Republican Palace represented for meetings there. Formally Saddam's center of government, it was now used as the offices of all the high brass of the Coalition Provisional Authority (CPA), including Paul Bremer.

Time went quickly, and evening approached. Art and I were both hungry, so we gathered our security detail and headed over to the Al-Rasheed to have dinner. The five of us—Art, myself, the two PSDs, and our driver—entered the hotel, passing through the military security posted at the entrance. The Al-Rasheed was much nicer than I expected and was appointed much like a four star hotel anywhere in the world. The lobby was spacious and furnished with stylish leather couches situated in clusters to provide individual socializing areas. It was nicely decorated with beautiful greenery and art. We found the restaurant fairly empty, and thus we were able to sit down immediately.

The driver of our security detail was Maisam, a fiftyish, white-haired and balding former petrochemical engineer. I mention Maisam because he imparted upon Art and me two separate, indelible impressions during our first day in Baghdad.

The first came as we parked our vehicle near the Republican Palace, exited and began to stride up to the enormous structure. Maisam had been step-for-step alongside when suddenly he stopped and stood quite still. I sensed that something was wrong; perhaps he was feeling ill. "Maisam, are you okay?" I asked. He stood there quite still for another moment or two and then traces of a grimaced smile were apparent. Finally he said, "I'm very sorry, but my knees began to shake quite uncontrollably. I am okay now."

Confusion must have been evident on my face. Maisam went on, "I have never been here before. This was very restricted land. If I had stood just here six months back, I would have certainly been put to death."

The impact of his countenance and words was overpowering. Maisam had needed to pause to reason away the acute peril he felt merely treading these grounds. It was another revelation, similar to that gained from a conversation months before with an Army major, about the heinous conditions in Iraq—conditions forcing such extreme and widespread adaptive behavior that the result was a dramatic alteration of the culture.

The other impression Maisam made concerned local logic and how it was being applied throughout the local neighborhoods of Baghdad.

We were perhaps an hour or so into dinner and a couple of bottles of pretty decent French wine when the conversation turned to the repercussions of the relatively recent bombings at the U.N. headquarters in Baghdad. Art and I felt it would turn the local Iraqis firmly against the insurgents and expressed as much.

Maisam had listened quietly for a while and then interjected, "I'm sorry but I believe you do not understand the typical Iraqi thinking. The belief in the street of this event is different." I was intrigued by Maisam's comments. As thoroughly as I felt I understood this region of the world—after all I had been doing business in the Middle East for the better part of twenty years—I was unprepared for his explanation.

"You must understand," Maisam admonished. "Many people in the local neighborhoods, even some of the well educated, believe the bombing of the U.N. buildings was ordered by the U.S. They believe it is a U.S. trick to make the Iraqis blame the insurgents."

I digested the meaning of his words in absolute silence. The Ensh Allah logic that led to driving at night without headlights made sense when compared to this logic. I realized this local logic created an ominous paradox for the United States and the coalition. If the horrible actions of the insurgents were to be ultimately blamed on the United States by virtue of this culturally rooted backward logic, then it would make the task of creating a democracy extremely difficult.

Maisam's clarification of the local logic, so perfectly rationalizing the recent U.N. calamity to Iraqi thinking, yet so farfetched to Western mentality, would serve as a gloomy harbinger of the struggle for the hearts and minds of the Iraqi people over the next few years of the violent insurgency.

No Oil for Food:
A Lesson in International Corruption

Iraq, or more specifically Babylon, is historically hailed as the origination of codified law. In 2000 BC, the ruler of Babylon developed a written system of laws known as the Code of Hammurabi. After working in Iraq for three years, I am convinced that Babylon must also have the dubious distinction as the creator of the concept of graft or accommodation.

Getting anything done at any level without accommodation is impossible in Iraq. All the locals engage in the ancient art of quid pro quo in practically every conceivable transaction. I soon learned that the reign of Saddam Hussein had escalated all pretense of the normal accommodation that exists throughout the world to full-blown fraud and dishonesty. It was in this environment of total accommodation immersion that my company was to experience a series of very unusual events operating within the United Nations Oil for Food program.

As background, the Oil for Food program was created in 1996 by the U.N. to allow Iraq to sell its embargoed oil specifically for food and medicines for the general population. To ensure the billions of dollars in oil sales allowed under the program went for these purposes, the U.N. had ostensibly established a strict inspection routine that purportedly comprised unscheduled and unannounced visits to inspect and ratify the medicines in the distribution warehouses in each of Iraq's eighteen governates.

In the spring of 2004, my new company was contracted by the Coalition Provisional Authority (CPA) to package and deliver some twelve million dollars worth of medicines and pharmaceuticals throughout Iraq. The funding for the procurement of the health care items on behalf of the Iraq Ministry of Health (MOH) came from proceeds allowed by the United Nations Oil for Food program. In the aftermath of the war, the CPA had usurped the control of these proceeds from the Baathists in charge. The items, some bought in the hundreds of thousands of doses, were a wide range of antivirals, antibiotics, steroids, and antipsychotics, along with condition-specific drugs such as insulin and intravenous fluids such as glucose and potassium chloride.

This supply was large enough to jumpstart the entire Iraqi medical care infrastructure which was woefully in need of these medicines.

The MOH deliveries for which we were contracted might have been routine, if anything in Iraq could be termed routine, if it wasn't for the fact that the deliveries to the governate warehouses were scheduled to occur before the handover of power. Governing power was scheduled to be transferred from the CPA, the temporary government created by General Tommy Franks and run by Paul Bremer, to the Interim Iraqi Government (IIG). Beginning with the anniversary of the invasion in April, there had been a marked increase in attacks by the insurgents on coalition forces, contractors, and even other Iraqis. The danger level spiraled upwards dramatically. It was widely believed that the increased level of attacks was a ploy by the insurgents to prevent the handover of power.

The ever-increasing danger level resulted in a near complete shutdown of the reconstruction activities. For weeks the roads nationwide were Code Red, meaning that contractors traveled at their own risk. If they were attacked, they had no promise of assistance from coalition forces. We were forced to deliver the pharmaceuticals under this dire threat scenario. As focused as we were on the extremely heightened danger levels, we had given very little thought to the facts and situation surrounding the essence of the shortage of these medicines and pharmaceuticals. The essence of this shortage would provide quite an awakening.

The medicines delivery operation began in late May of 2004. The atmosphere was tense. Of course, it was hot. As early as March, temperatures begin reaching triple digits. The heat and humidity made the dangers seem even more pronounced. The Western security teams that we had arranged to guard the shipments throughout Iraq would not operate due to the Code Red road situation. In order to stay on schedule, one of our local Iraqi trucking contractors hired former Republican Guard officers to travel with and guard the expensive supplies.

The first shipment to the Baghdad warehouse, operated by a company hired during Saddam's regime, contained a small portion of medicines requiring refrigeration. It was important to transfer these items immediately upon delivery. Although we had made thousands of deliveries around Iraq up to that point, this very first delivery to one of the main Baghdad warehouses was very memorable.

The large truck departed the Baghdad International Airport (BIAP) staging area late in the morning and arrived at the warehouse designated as MOH Warehouse #1. As prearranged, the security team of former Republican Guard soldiers escorted the truck to the warehouse, confirmed the safety of the security situation, and made preparations to depart.

Accompanying the truck and security team to the warehouse was Abdul, one of Logenix's local Baghdad staff. As the caravan arrived at the warehouse, they were met by the manager, a Mr. Al Salam of the company Chimidia. Al Salam immediately approached Abdul and said, "The truck can not be offloaded. You must leave here immediately."

Surprised by this information, Abdul called my manager at the time, Martyn, who was in our Green Zone office. Abdul relayed to Martyn, "The manager of the warehouse will not take delivery!"

Martyn was also surprised. The delivery had been pre-coordinated. Martyn instructed Abdul to explain to Al Salam that this was the important delivery for the Iraq MOH that had been prearranged only days prior. Unimpressed, Al Salam reiterated his instructions and then hurriedly left the premises. Abdul then again called Martyn to explain. In order to sort out the situation, Martyn ordered Abdul and the truck to remain at the warehouse while he made telephone calls to sort out this oddly developing situation.

Martyn then called Alicia, the American CPA official overseeing this effort, who in turn called the Director General, Mr. Talibee, of Chimidia. Calling Martyn back, Alicia reported more strange news.

Talibee had told Alicia that Al Salam told him just minutes before that there was no truck at the warehouse. Al Salam also stated he was present at the warehouse and had been all morning. Thoroughly perplexed by this news from Alicia, Martyn then phoned Abdul back. Abdul protested that Al Salam was not at the warehouse and that, of course, he and the truck were still there. In a following series of phone calls, between Martyn and Talibee, the situation began to escalate. First, Talibee asked for the truck number and description. Martyn, starting to become suspicious, refused to give Talibee the information.

Next, Talibee stated that the warehouse refrigeration section was being repaired and the truck would have to return to deliver the items that required refrigeration. Then, and proving extremely suspicious later, Talibee strangely accused Martyn of changing the truck information given at the time of the delivery arrangement. That was the same delivery information of which Al Salam had denied any knowledge.

During the time frame of the initial call to Alicia and the following calls to Talibee, some disturbing news came to light. Abdul, with Al Salam having disappeared, had begun investigating the warehouse and had found the refrigeration area to be in good working order. There were no signs of repairs.

Perhaps two hours had elapsed since the truck first arrived at the warehouse when very alarming news was received. Martyn was informed that our security team, as they departed the warehouse, had very narrowly missed being attacked. There had been a RPG attack, only a few hundred meters from warehouse #1, on a truck immediately in front of our returning security detail. The RPG attack was followed by a hail of small arms fire. Were it not for Martyn's orders to remain at the warehouse, the truck attacked would have been ours.

It was at this point, Martyn told me later, that the hair began to stand up on the back of his neck. Something wasn't right.

Given the extremely odd events and actions, we all firmly believe that RPG attack was meant to destroy our truck. More pointedly, it was directed at the medicines it was carrying. Al Salam's insistence that the truck depart immediately, his lying about the truck and his location, Talibee's lying about the broken refrigeration unit and his strange questions about the truck amounted to a chilling chain of circumstantial evidence. If Marcia Clark had possessed such evidence, she'd have gotten O. J. for sure.

"Why?" was the overriding question. Why would these Iraqis want to prevent these valuable and much-needed supplies from being delivered? I think the answer lies within other informational insights gathered as we continued the MOH deliveries throughout Iraq.

During a later delivery, Martyn struck up a conversation with a local worker in that warehouse. The worker, demonstrating intimate knowledge of the past operations, put forth information in decent English that succinctly put into perspective the immense level of corruption, and collaboration, enveloping the U.N. Oil for Food program.

The worker stated that there had been no new medicines delivered to that warehouse in years. He explained that the same batch of supplies was shipped from one warehouse to another to coincide with the "random" U.N. inspectors' visits. The outdated and shabby supplies then on hand had expired many years before. This would seem to indicate that other than one small group of medicines, purchased years before, there had been no drugs bought with Oil for Food funds in quite some time. This insight was among the very first—none of the illegal allegations surrounding the Oil for Food Program had yet been reported by any of the world media. Essentially, my company was the first to stumble upon, although very accidentally, the billion dollar scam.

There is no way both Al Salam and Talibee couldn't have known the situation. I'm sure they were in it up to their eyeballs. We believe both were involved in trying to extend the cover up of one of history's great scams.

The real question, as we came to view it, was how far up the U.N. chain this international hoax extended. It seems implausible that any scam with this amount of money—billions were involved—wouldn't have reached far up the authority chain at the U.N. Benon Sevan, the U.N. administrator of the program, seemed involved for sure. Ultimately, but only after a series of investigations left him no option, he resigned. Was Kofi Annan involved? With the amount of money and the degree of complicity so clearly evident, it seems a real stretch of the imagination to me that he was not at least aware.

When accommodation is left unchecked by ethical or legal boundaries, the corrupt scam that the Oil for Food program represents was an extreme but, unfortunately, natural progression.

Sign of the Times

The U.N. does a lot of good in the world, but I think it's no stretch to say it needs a major overhaul. My experiences in Afghanistan and Iraq with U.N. corruption were my most direct, but I have heard rumblings for years. As a result of the Oil for Food scam both the Volker Commission and a confidential report issued by the U.N.'s internal watchdog, the Office of Internal Oversight Services (OIOS), delivered scathing denouncements of the U.N.'s financial dealings. Terms like "systematic abuse" and "pattern of corrupt practices" were abundant in the findings. Nearly one third of all U.N. procurement contracts were charged to have involved waste, corruption, or other inexcusable irregularities.

On American Soil:
A Culmination of Lessons

To this point, I have focused almost exclusively on my experience in the International business environment. However, the lessons I learned in my international adventures have had practical applications in my business dealings within the American business market. The following experiences involving the volatile aftermath of the sale of my company in 1996, the multi-million dollar exit negotiations that paved the way for my departure from the new entity in January of 1998, and the head shaking legal battle that resulted in 2001 are a testament to that fact.

The acquisition of my company was one in a series of acquisitions, in financial terms called a roll up, by a financial entity called International Logistics Limited (ILL) en route to an Initial Public Offering (IPO) of stock. In the go-go euphoria of the late nineties, all the principals associated with the ILL roll up were completely obsessed with the instant personal riches an IPO would bring. A growing culture of greed that became infamous in business circles of the late 1990s—coined by Alan Greenspan as "infectious" —would encompass my company within months. Looking back, it was pretty inevitable.

As time went by—albeit in sharp contrast to the financial wunderkind at Simon & Sons—I felt the financial standing of the combined ILL entities made IPO riches a real fantasy. I saw a logic at play that I perceived to be somewhere between the Ensh Allah mindset and that of the Masai guide. The corporate logic needed both the blind faith of Ensh Allah and the absence of any reasoning that had led the Masai guide to his actions. The logic was cultural.

Hand-in-hand with that thought, I realized the dominant culture being developed was, as an analogy, a blend of Saudi-like arrogance and Soviet bureaucracy. The new owners loved meetings and loved giving orders, any orders. I hated frivolous meetings and, like most entrepreneurs, didn't like taking orders from bureaucratic suits that did not have a clue about what they were doing.

As I alluded to in the confrontation with Lenin, corporate culture can be as varied as it is within countries. Approaches, attitudes, and values of different companies can be as different as the cultures of Nigeria and Thailand. I had realized that the cultural differences between my company and the acquiring company, ILL, were just as diametrically opposed. Even worse, I felt the ideals held by those within ILL were just as misguided and would be as disastrous as those of Lenin.

Within six months of the sale, I decided to leave the company so a negotiation regarding my guaranteed contract was necessary. The beginning of those negotiations started unpromisingly. Months rolled by as I waited for a bona fide offer from the ILL CEO.

I had developed a theory—based upon my realizations of the ILL culture—of the directions in which the situation might progress. If ILL were operating in good faith, which I was not expecting, they would send a proposal before any meeting on the subject. If they were trying to be disingenuous, they would spring an offer on me at a meeting and attempt to get an immediate agreement.

A meeting in late November was arranged in Denver, the second headquarters office of this now billion-dollar entity. As expected, no proposal preceded the meeting. My negotiating agenda was set. It was going to be no different than buying a carpet in a Middle East souk. I was also going to watch for leverage, and I knew I needed to be careful about the perception of that leverage

When the CEO and I finally sat down, he put forth an offer to supplant my contract. It was low on cash and high on stock warrants—ILL's favorite worthless enticement. Stock warrants, really nothing more than a valueless promise, were the prime ILL carrot that I never understood other people's attraction to. Any warrant offer from ILL was a prayer, in their case a huge one, that ILL would *someday* become a public company. Given the company culture I had witnessed, I was certain that prayer would go unanswered. But I had discovered my leverage.

I countered the offer with a reasonable cash-only buyout along with a much shorter non-compete agreement. ILL management was worried that I would leave and take all the profitable business with me, so they were determined to have me wrapped up in a non-compete. My offer was given no heed. The CEO's response was that negotiations were over. As I sat there, I couldn't help but smile to myself as I plotted out the lesson I was about to give the CEO of this billion dollar company. He was going to be as soundly thumped as I had been by the Indians in Hyderabad, and he wouldn't have jetlag to blame.

I left the office and flew back to Washington where I retained legal counsel. Within a week, I had the cash financial terms I wanted and the shorter non-compete. The cash offer had more than tripled for a non-compete that was almost 40 percent reduced in duration. Like the hotel arcade shop owner in Indonesia, the CEO's insincere negotiating tactics actually cost him leverage. Once lawyers were involved, he was back-pedaling constantly, as he could not support his offer in Denver. Also, because he was focused on the certainty of an IPO, he would lose on the real issue.

The most important part of the negotiation—and the strongest case I can make for the development of intuition as a business guide—regarded a minimum price guarantee for my ILL stock, an additional benefit received from the sale of my company. Trading stock warrants—valueless absent an IPO—for this guarantee had been my leverage epiphany in the Denver meeting. This minimum price guarantee would turn out to be the coup de grace of the negotiation as it would be the only legal value anyone could ever claim for ILL stock. From a negotiating standpoint, ILL's CEO needed much more exposure to the world, especially the markets, souks, and arcades of the Middle East and Asia.

In the skewed, greed-based logic of those within ILL, the thinking of the day was that I had been outfoxed. I gave up the warrants and the highly prized rights to more ILL stock that would come from an IPO. My impressions of the culture and the greed-based logic left me with an almost tangible intuitive sense that this company could easily fail. However, my belief was completely counter to the popular, financial thinking of the time. The path I followed, from leaving to turning down the various stock enticements, was seen as impossibly naïve.

It would only take two short years for my position to be borne out. Unfortunately, my negotiating success would also provide the basis for a rather implausible American legal experience.

In just eighteen months, my old company would go from being the prize jewel in the crown of ILL, renamed Geologistics, to one of its worst performers. The culture of the company had completely changed from a dynamic, results-oriented organization to an organization focused on money as the be all and end all. Unfortunately, this attitude was all too pervasive in American business at the time.

For the fiscal year of 1999, the annual Securities & Exchange Commission (SEC) filing for Geologistics announced a loss—a whopping $49 million net loss for the year. By the time of their mid-year SEC filing in 2000, the loss had escalated to $27 million for just the first six months of that year. Total stockholders deficit was listed at $71 million. The downward financial spiral was now a headlong plummet. The stock guarantee I had negotiated would be worthless if Geologistics went bankrupt. And, to me that was exactly where it looked like they were headed.

On the very first day of the expiration of my two and a half year non-compete, I executed what was termed in the separation agreement as my "put." This was notification to Geologistics that they now had to pay me the guaranteed price for my stock. The stock was now otherwise worthless. My agreement was, indeed, golden. Geologistics by then had a new CEO who responded to my put—the former CEO had been fired the year before. The new CEO suggested that I might have violated my non-compete restrictions. He suggested that I should fly to California, the latest headquarters of Geologistics, to discuss the issue with him.

Geologistics was in real financial trouble, and it appeared they were about to try to wiggle out of the stock guarantee. I immediately contacted the lawyer who had worked on my separation agreement. Thus began a series of letters between my lawyers and Geologistics. In due course, Geologistics sent a letter offering me approximately twenty-five dollars for my stock. The offer wasn't even in the right financial *galaxy*. It was clear to me we were headed to arbitration.

When I had agreed to the arbitration clause in my separation agreement, I had no preconceived notions. Its relevance was to preclude regular court proceedings to settle any and all disputes. I only knew arbitration was a pseudo-court. If anything, avoiding court struck me as a sound idea. I was to learn that "kangaroo court" was a much more appropriate and fitting description of the arbitration process. Those in the right are far better off in front of a real judge with real rules and power.

The thirteen months it took for the arbitration process to unravel were marked by every legal delay tactic possible by the Geologistics lawyers. It took almost six months to obtain a statement from them of just how I had materially breached my separation agreement. It seemed clear to my lawyers and me the tactics were driven by their precarious financial situation.

My lead litigation lawyer, Mark, quickly made evident his disdain for arbitration as a legal forum. Preparing me for the Kabuki theatre—his term for arbitration—he explained that in his opinion, if you're guilty you want to be in arbitration, but if you're innocent you want to be in a real court. It was clear that, with the unscrupulous case Geologistics intended to present, they were presenting it in the right forum.

Mark also pointed out another huge flaw of arbitration—a flaw he believed fatally corrupted the legal process. Mark explained that the sad reality was that arbitrators want to be chosen again, and happy past litigants would probably select them in future arbitrations. In my case, the probability that I would be involved in future arbitration was slim, as it is for any individual. The arbiters predisposition would lean toward Geologistics, a corporation almost certain to be involved in future arbitrations.

If for even one moment you thought that accommodation was only an overseas issue, think again. This was accommodation in its purest, most sophisticated form. The arbitrators understood the unspoken accommodation of return business as if they had been schooled by my Kazak ministry buddy. Accommodation exists in the United States at this level, in this general form as an almost invisible game of quid pro quo.

I began to realize I was in a legal process, right here in the United States of America, that was much closer to George's Thailand experience than I had ever thought possible. I had not known—and probably wouldn't have believed—that arbitration was so fundamentally flawed. To say the least, and certainly offering concrete proof that law of the land concerns are prevalent everywhere, I should have looked into the facts of arbitration before allowing it to be a condition of my separation agreement. I felt like Rod must have when he learned of the incongruous and hopelessly biased nature of the Saudi law governing the accident with the hajji.

Waiting for the arbitration trial, my lawyers and I received some startling news. My lawyers had been sent a copy of a written affidavit, signed by Sergey, in which he vowed that each and every ludicrous charge Geologistics had finally put forth, concerning my violations of the non-compete agreement, was true. This document changed everything—instead of a slam-dunk win, I could actually lose.

Although we had not spoken in over a year, I telephoned Sergey that weekend and we spent almost two hours talking. Over the telephone that day, Sergey explained that Geologistics had applied some serious financial pressure to get his affidavit. He admitted he regretted his actions, although Geologistics' pressure had left him no real option.

I asked if he would like to meet in Europe to discuss the messy situation. He said, "Of course," and we decided to meet in Paris. The two days we spent in Paris were just like old times. We enjoyed ourselves thoroughly in the cafés, restaurants, and nightclubs of the city and developed a simple plan. Sergey would simply deny understanding the first affidavit since it had been presented to him only in English. He would then sign a second affidavit, also translated into Russian, stating that the charges Geologistics had put forth were false. It was brilliant—and so very Russian.

The morning of the first day of the hearings finally arrived. I met Mark and his Harvard Law–trained co-counsel, Stephanie, in the lobby of the downtown

Marriott in Chicago. Within a ten-minutes walk, we arrived at the law offices being used for the arbitration hearing. It was a beautiful July day with hardly a cloud in the sky. We were shown to a large and imposing corner conference room on the fortieth floor. It was approximately fifty feet long with a very large conference table that must have been over thirty feet in length. The room had floor to ceiling windows and had a stunning panoramic vista of the Chicago area.

The stage was impressively set for what was going to be a stressful and tense three days. During that time, Geologistics brought in a half dozen people trying to make their case. Mark had been right. It was a Kabuki theatre, and it became so from the opening moments.

Mark and Stephanie were practically drooling at the prospect of cross-examining the new Geologistics CEO. To our surprise, the first order of business was to deal with the fact that the new CEO had not shown. The chief counsel of Geologistics had arrived to act as the CEO's surrogate. It was not supposed to happen that way—but this was Kabuki Theatre.

The Geologistics chief counsel took the witness chair. Mark proceeded to ask the routine initial questions each witness would undergo: background, current position, etc. The perfunctory questions to the chief counsel naturally included those regarding his legal training and licensing in the United States. When Mark asked about his license to practice law, Geologistics' chief legal counsel testified he had none.

For a moment even Mark was speechless. The arbitrators were stunned. Here's a guy representing himself as a lawyer, attempting to pull a legal fast one by trying to shield the main witness, and he's *not licensed* by any state bar association in the United States. Incredible as it seemed—the Geologistics "lawyer" was just shooed from the witness chair.

That's the way it started, and this sorry excuse for a legal proceeding continued along these lines.

Geologistics, for some reason I could never fathom, was claiming Sergey did not speak very good English. I spoke almost no Russian, yet Sergey and I had built a multimillion dollar business in Russia and the CIS. You would think this claim would not pass a sniff test, but in this forum it did.

Hence, Geologistics wanted a translator for Sergey's testimony. While the request was laughable, it would serve to underscore Sergey's upcoming testimony regarding the first affidavit that was given to him only in English. Unlike in the Vienna situation, we had no need to hire our own translator. Sergey, unbeknownst to Geologistics lawyers, would supply any missed allusion in translation. Sergey was, in a sense, our confirmation of translation.

Sergey's testimony and its translation had an unusual and humorous side. Arbitration, copying real legal proceedings, is given to formal interaction. Every statement or question is usually preceded by formally addressing a person. The arbitrators are addressed as "Your Honor." The lawyers, witnesses, defendants, and plaintiffs are all addressed as Mr. or Ms. This formality, and especially its frequency, was about to deliver some slapstick humor to three of us in the room.

In Paris, Sergey had explained that the name of Geologistics's lead lawyer, when spoken aloud, sounded *exactly* like the Russian slang word for shit. When it was Sergey's turn to testify, the translator—perhaps the best I had ever witnessed—had noticeably blanched when first introduced to the Geologistics lawyer. His eyes had completely given away the despair he obviously felt upon realizing the name he would have to repeat throughout the proceedings. The lawyer's name would come up in Sergey's almost two-hour testimony and cross-examination at least fifty times. Both the translator and Sergey tried continually to pronounce the name differently. As if right out of a vaudeville act as the straight man of a comedy duo, Geologistics's lawyer kept politely correcting the purposeful mispronunciations. Each time his name was mispronounced, he would smile reassuringly and essentially say, "No, that's Mr. Shit, S-H-I-T."

With Sergey's testimony underway, the unmistakable timing of the constant snickering noticeably flustered the translator. He knew Sergey knew what was going on, and after my inability to stifle my chuckling, he knew I knew. It also became clear that the arbitrators were aware that something was going on. The only one completely in the dark was the lawyer—Mr. Shit himself.

This communications situation was every bit as funny as the Sudanese "rain" situation with Lee and right up there with Debbie's flawed Russian introduction in the Kazak restaurant. Given any exposure to communications issues in a multi-lingual environment, the lawyer surely would have figured there must be *some* reason for the stifled laughter in that boardroom. His lack of awareness led to a distinct sense that his grasp of the legal issues might not be any better than his grasp of the communications element in the boardroom. In the end, it was a subtle but distinct blow to his competency.

As the questioning continued, the rhythm of answers to questions fell out of sync. Often, Sergey would answer questions posed in English before the translator finished translating. After the tenth or so such incident, the head arbitrator stopped the proceedings. He looked at me and asked, "Mr. Cruse, do you speak fluent Russian?" I replied that I did not. "In what language" he continued, "did you and Mr. Kuzminykh do business for five years?" "English," I replied. He looked at Sergey. Without any translation

Sergey nodded and said, "English." With that Sergey was dismissed from the stand and all testimony regarding Sergey, including both affidavits, was thrown out. The entire day and countless hours of legal cost were tossed away as if it never happened.

Incredibly, the case dragged on. Before closing arguments, a short recess was held. The Geologistics side was very late returning. When they did, they tabled a settlement offer. It was very handsome, but I was in no mood for anything short of total victory.

Mark cautioned me to think about the very real prospects of bankruptcy court. A banker prior to getting his law degree, Mark was well-versed in reading financial balance sheets—and those of Geologistics were dire. Even Geologistics lawyers had been making strong innuendoes concerning their client's poor financial health. Emphatically, Mark cautioned me again about the capriciousness of arbitration.

Mark had been right every step of the way. I had to admit, given all the shenanigans from the Geologistics side, I was stunned the arbitration process had proceeded to this point. Stubbornly ignoring all this, I turned down the offer. We returned for closing arguments.

Sitting down, Mark sarcastically remarked that I would enjoy learning about bankruptcy court. Suddenly, all Mark's cautioning hit home. I was so geared up that I was not thinking clearly. Once again Howard and the fur hat lady came to mind, and I realized the leverage here was not as I was perceiving it. Geologistics precarious financial position actually gave them leverage. I had won the battle, but I could lose the war if they went into bankruptcy. This understanding of leverage, and the correct perception of it, was critical.

All of this went through my mind within seconds of Mark's comment. Intuitively, I sensed that Mark was right. I wrote a note and slid it across to the unlicensed chief counsel—it was over.

Well, not quite. As the unlicensed chief counsel and I stood up, he told me that Geologistics could not pay me immediately. It would take months to come up with the cash. Looking him in the eye, I realized just how close Geologistics, this billion-dollar company with nearly three hundred offices in over thirty countries, was to financial collapse. I had made the right decision.

Not twenty minutes later, with the settlement in writing and signed, we were all headed for airplanes. I didn't know it then, but the next week would be spent wrangling over a confidentiality clause that Geologistics wanted included in the final agreement. I didn't like it, but I understood it. As in the Bosnian issue, the main goal was accomplished. Avoiding the loss of face on the other side was part of the means to attaining the intended goal.

Reflecting on the wrangling surrounding the sale of my company, I realized just how much my cadre of lessons had assisted me—even in a domestic business environment.

Oh, and in case I forgot to mention it, there never was an IPO, and I got the money.

Epilogue

When I embarked on my career, I wanted international travel, excitement, and glamour—well, two out of three isn't bad. The phrase "Be careful for what you wish" was never more appropriate as I ran for planes in the midst of civil insurrections or lay violently ill in some remote African hotel room.

On a trip to Lebanon in July of 2006, still globetrotting and racking up adventures in the pursuit of business for Logenix, I missed being stranded in Beirut for perhaps a month or more by a mere matter of days. In a skirmish between the Israelis and Hezbollah that nearly evolved into a full-scale war, the airport became one of the early targets. This made traditional commercial air departure impossible for over a month.

Learning about the outbreak of hostilities, I was amazed by the realization that that the imminent danger I found myself in so many times in my travels had increased, rather than subsided, around the world. Both Afghanistan and Iraq were probably more *potentially* dangerous than any other countries I had encountered, and the location I had just departed, Lebanon, obviously remained a very, very volatile place.

This assessment of the very dicey travel conditions existent around the world brought back an image from my arrival in Lebanon only two weeks prior. Looking around the airport immigration line as I entered Beirut, I had noticed a twenty-something American standing in the immigration line looking for all the world like I had twenty years ago. Maybe not that clueless, but close. Something about the appearance of this young man had spurred an unmistakable wave of déjà vu, bringing to mind my first arrival into Saudi Arabia.

Thinking about my near miss in Lebanon and that wave of déjà vu at the airport, I was struck by the fact that all the experiences and lessons I had gleaned first in Saudi Arabia and later in places like India, Thailand, and Russia were so fresh and remained so profoundly pertinent. Through it all, at the very foundation, were the lessons on culture with the intrinsically linked insights on logic and maintaining face. Thus, the culturally rooted lessons on accommodation, communications, negotiation, and jurisprudence, remained priceless. Without a basic understanding of a country's, or even a corporation's culture, business pursuits could at the very least offend or, at worst, come to a grinding halt. Also, in such uncharted country and business environments, I realized intuition and a simple approach to problem solving were as valuable and necessary as they had always been to me.

Without question, these rules I had come to operate by were essential to the entrepreneurial achievement I had attained. Three companies, two in the United States and one in Russia, had enjoyed remarkable success due to the lessons I had picked up and implemented along the way.

In twenty years of globetrotting, so much has changed, yet nothing is different. The lessons I learned in my years of international travel are universal through time and place. I offer them here as a harbinger of success to those interested in engaging in the intriguing, fascinating, yet risk-plagued arena of global business.

About the Author

Ron Cruse was born and raised in Oklahoma. His mother, a Scottish WWII war bride, filled him with stories of the world at an early age and his father, an educational psychologist, instilled in him a 'do it right' ethical compass. Exhibiting the classic earmarks of an entrepreneur, Cruse spent a good part of his school years challenging authority. He attended Villanova University, receiving a top flight education, yet later would face the reality that the down-in-the-trenches, practical training necessary to navigate the real world of international commerce was not to be found in any college curriculum.

After graduation Mr. Cruse made his way to New York City and eventually landed a job in the international shipping industry. On a meteoric career path in his late twenties he found himself traveling the world learning the entrepreneurial skills that would build three remarkably successful multi-million dollar international companies. The course of the next twenty years would have Cruse conducting business in over 80 countries while traveling nearly two million miles worldwide.

In 1986 he founded his own company, Matrix, along with three partners. Cruse was soon traveling to every hotspot around the globe, countries like Pakistan, Somalia, Nigeria, Burma, and Egypt to name just a few, growing his business. As testament to Cruse's business acumen, the dazzling two thousand percent plus growth of his company was first recognized in 1991 by *INC Magazine*. Matrix was listed #81 of *INC's* 500 Fastest Growing Private Companies in the United States.

In 1992 Cruse entered Russia just months after the collapse of the Former Soviet Union. Realizing the entrepreneurial opportunities, he organized one of the very first US-Russian Joint Venture Companies. Matrix became immersed in every major U.S. Government activity in the New Republics; from weapons dismantlement to nuclear reactor modernization to refugee assistance during the Chechan conflict. Cruse's life became a swirl of KGB, CIA, and underworld intrigue while dealing with practically every top-secret installation of the Former Soviet Union. By 1995, he was a recognized expert and speaker on the business infrastructure of the republics comprising the

New Independent States (NIS). In 1996, Cruse and Matrix were profiled in the *American Shipper*, a transportation industry monthly, as representative of the leading edge of the transport industry in the New Republics.

The high profile business foothold in the new republics, six offices in five republics comprising the largest privately held freight forwarding operation in the NIS, and the lucrative profits garnered there led to acquisition. In late 1996 Matrix, by then an 85 million dollar company, was bought by an investment group led by the former Secretary of the Treasury, William Simon.

In 2001 Cruse founded his third entrepreneurial venture, Logenix International, Inc. Also achieving meteoric growth, by 2005 Logenix grew to be a 20 million dollar company. Logenix has assisted in the rebuilding of Afghanistan, the reconstruction of Iraq, and is an integral facilitator supporting health and humanitarian assistance efforts across Africa and Asia. Profiled in *Forbes Magazine*, *Financial Times*, and in industry magazines such as *Logistics Today*, Cruse and his new company continue to be involved in world headline making events.

Cruse's career journey is the inspiration for the book, *LIES, BRIBES, & PERILS: Lessons for the REAL Challenges of International Business*. In the book, Cruse relates profound insights and simple lessons learned from a unique cast of characters around the world; lessons that can be a prime determinant of business success or failure. This book provides an education not to be found in any classroom in the United States.

Breinigsville, PA USA
31 January 2010
231672BV00006B/124/P